MICHAEL MATTHEWS

8TH AUGUST. 1981

ROLLS-ROYCE SILVER CLOUD

Osprey AutoHistory

ROLLS-ROYCE SILVER CLOUD

Phantom V, VI and Bentley S series, Continental

GRAHAM ROBSON

Published in 1980 by Osprey Publishing Limited,
12–14 Long Acre, London WC2 9LP
Member company of the George Philip Group

United States distribution by

Osceola, Wisconsin 54020, USA

British Library Cataloguing in Publication Data

Robson, Graham
Rolls-Royce Silver Cloud.
(Osprey autohistory).
1. Silver Cloud automobile
I. Title
629.22′22 TL215.S/
ISBN 0-85045-380-1

Editor Tim Parker
Associate Michael Sedgwick
Photography Mirco Decet
Design Fred Price

Filmset and printed in England by
BAS Printers Limited, Over Wallop, Hampshire

Contents

Chapter 1 Derby and Crewe – the Heritage

Authors more distinguished than myself have often pointed out that the Silver Cloud and S series models announced in 1955 were the last of the 'traditional' type of Rolls-Royce. The Silver Shadow series which replaced them in 1965 embraces an entirely different design philosophy, and the Phantom VI of the 1970s was really no more than an expansion of the Silver Cloud's layout. Even the Silver Shadow, however, shows continuity with the earlier car, for in its original condition it used the same engine and transmission, and both projects were developed under the leadership of that well-respected engineer, Harry Grylls. The tradition, therefore, which inspired the creation of the Silver Cloud deserves study.

It is a tradition now well and truly documented, which stretches back to 1904, when a 10 hp prototype, based on the design of a French Decauville, was built in Manchester by Henry Royce and his two apprentices. Royce was introduced to the Hon. Charles Rolls later that year, and concluded a marketing agreement with him in December, whereby Rolls and Co. agreed to take all the cars produced by Royce, and sell them as Rolls-Royce models. In 1906 the Rolls-Royce Company was founded.

After the usual prolific period enjoyed by almost every British car maker in Edwardian times, Rolls-Royce announced the magnificent 40/50 model in 1906, and settled down to a patrician 'one-model' policy. In the meantime, they outgrew their Manchester premises, and moved into the new Derby factory in July 1908. It was not until October 1922, however, that they were ready to break this policy, announce the new 'small' Rolls-Royce—the 20 hp model—and set in train a series of mechanical developments which have genuine links with the first Silver Clouds.

Central to the design of the original Twenty was the all-new in-line pushrod operated overhead valve six-cylinder engine, originally with bore and stroke of 76·2 × 114·3 mm, and a

In the early 1950s, Rolls-Royce re-styled the tail of the 'standard steel' saloons, lengthening them and increasing the boot capacity, and brought in performance improvements. The Bentley became known as the 'R type' (the Silver Dawn was never re-named)

WMC 84

swept volume of 3127 cc. The *really* important dimension in this engine, however, was that of 4·15 inches between the centre lines of neighbouring cylinder bores (except between No. 3 and No. 4 cylinders). This was both a recognisable 'signature' for the long-running family which was to develop, and an important restriction to the engine's eventual growth.

Between the wars, the 20 hp became the 20/25 hp model in 1929, the 25/30 hp derivative in 1936, and gave way to the Wraith in 1938. A sporting development of the 20/25, the $3\frac{1}{2}$-litre Bentley ('The Silent Sports Car'), came on the scene in 1933 following the take over of that famous, but bankrupt, firm. The $3\frac{1}{2}$-litre became a $4\frac{1}{4}$-litre in 1936, and was about to be replaced by

Above *Rolls-Royce began making cars at their Crewe factory in 1946. Previous Rolls-Royce cars had been built at Derby. The Crewe building was a World War Two 'shadow factory' which originally assembled aero engines*

Left *An H. J. Mulliner coachbuilt bodyshell on the Bentley Mk VI chassis showing unmistakable signs of the way in which the styling of the later S series cars developed. This shell was of all-steel construction*

From 1946, and for the first time in their history, Rolls-Royce began to build complete cars with what became known as a 'standard steel' bodyshell by Pressed Steel. The first 'standard steel' model was the Mk VI Bentley of 1946, and the Rolls-Royce Silver Dawn derivative followed in 1949. This example, like so many Silver Dawns, had left-hand-drive, and was destined for an export market

the Mk V in 1939 when the Second World War broke out.

Along the way, Rolls-Royce had espoused the Hispano-Suiza type of mechanically clutched four-wheel brake servo (from 1923), synchromesh gears (from 1932), the coil spring independent front suspension (from 1935 on the Phantom III, from 1938 on the Wraith, and from 1939 on the Mark V Bentley), all of which would have an influence on postwar design.

However, two other developments were critical, one relating to the way in which the cars would be built, and one as to the location of the factory. Before and during the Second World War, Rolls-Royce, already pre-eminent in the aero-engine business, expanded these interests enormously, and the great success of the Merlin vee-12 aero engine and the gas turbine engines which were to follow it meant that the Derby factory was really needed to build nothing else. The decision was therefore taken to build postwar Rolls-Royce and Bentley cars in a 'shadow' factory at Crewe, which had been building aero engines up to that time.

Even before the onset of war in 1939, Rolls-Royce Ltd. had seen that the day of the coachbuilt body shell was now coming to an end. The Second World War formed a watershed in the Company's affairs. Up until 1939 Rolls-Royce never built a complete car; after 1945 the vast majority of their products were completely assembled at Crewe using 'standard steel' pressed-steel bodies.

In the meantime, the great demands of the Armed Forces had led Rolls-Royce to initiate the design of a range of four-, six- and eight-cylinder engines, all of which could use a series of common components, share some of the same machine tool equipment, and which could rely to some extent on the bare bones of the existing and long-established six-cylinder engine. That important 4·15 inch dimension between adjacent cylinder centres was to be retained, though many other aspects of the design were new.

It is worth diverting here to recall the progressive changes made to the engine itself. Originally it had had a 3·0 inch bore and a 4·5 inch stroke (76·2 × 114·3 mm), which gave a capacity of 3127 cc, and neither the cylinder centre dimension nor the stroke was ever changed. The bore was increased to 3·25 inch (82·55 mm) and the capacity to 3669 cc for the 20/25 and for the original

Above *The massive and elegant Silver Wraith model, first put on sale in 1947, was the true ancestor of the Phantom V. This James Young creation is seen outside its creator's premises*

Right *One of the most exciting post-war Bentleys of all was the original R type Continental, with two-door fastback coachwork by H. J. Mulliner*

$3\frac{1}{2}$-litre Bentley, and to 3·5 inch (88·9 mm) with a capacity of 4257 cc for the 25/30, Wraith, $4\frac{1}{4}$ and Mark V Bentleys of 1936–1939. For the rationalized series of engines, the existing bore and stroke was not to be changed, but a different type of cylinder head and breathing—with a large overhead inlet valve, and a side-mounted exhaust valve—was adopted. The three engines—coded B40, B60, B80—had capacities of 2838 cc, 4257 cc and 5675 cc.

The stage was now set for postwar production of Rolls-Royce and Bentley cars to begin. In the meantime certain wide-ranging decisions had been taken. It had been decided that due to social and economic conditions, there was no longer a viable market for really big-engined cars. The vast, incredibly costly and complex vee-12 Phantom III was not re-introduced, and for a time there was no Rolls-Royce car in production. At first, Crewe concentrated on building Mark VI Bentleys—which were effectively, if not when it came to detail, updated Wraith/Mark V chassis combined with the new $4\frac{1}{4}$-litre B60-type of engine, fitted with a standard steel bodyshell provided by the Pressed Steel Co. Ltd.

The postwar Silver Wraith, similar in many ways to the Mark VI but with coachbuilt bodyshells provided by approved specialists, followed in 1947, and the Rolls-Royce Silver Dawn (a less powerful but otherwise badge-engineered Mark VI) came along in 1949. Effectively, the cars built at Crewe at the end of the 1940s conformed to a one-model—or at least a one-model-range—policy, and not even the 'potentates-only' Phantom IV of 1950–56 (of which only sixteen were built, with the B80 5·7-litre engine) really changed that.

The basic design was eventually to run from 1946 to 1955 (or to 1959, if the last of the Silver Wraith cars is considered), during which the range was further expanded, and the engine further improved. Changes made to the Mark VI standard steel saloon—turning it into the R type or B7 variety—were confined to reshaping and enlarging the luggage compartment in the tail. This, incidentally, provided a logical development from the original shape to the model which was to replace it in 1955, but was nothing compared to the series of sleek, two-door, coupé Continentals made available from 1952. Helped by the most powerful types of Rolls-Royce engines, here with a vengeance was a return to 'The Silent Sports Car' which Rolls-Royce had built so effectively in the 1930s.

Engine changes were confined to further tuning and enlargement to keep abreast with performance standards in general, and to endow the Continentals with really high top speeds for European journeys. Still without altering the 4·15 inch dimension between cylinder centres, or without changing the stroke, there were two further enlargements. In 1951, the engines were enlarged to 4566 cc with the aid of $3\frac{5}{8}$ in (92·07 mm) cylinder bores, and from 1954, for the Continentals only, that bore was further increased to $3\frac{3}{4}$ inch (95·25 mm), and the capacity to 4887 cc. It proved to be the last change which could be made with any certainty to a layout whose basic dimensions had been conceived in 1919 and put into production in 1922.

By the beginning of the 1950s, with Britain ready to climb out of its period of postwar austerity, with car sales booming all over the world, and with demand for its cars higher than ever before, Rolls-Royce were ready for the next big step forward. Indeed, Harry Grylls and his engineering team had been thinking about their future for some time. The Silver Cloud and S series Bentleys of 1955 were the result.

Chapter 2
Shaping the Cloud

For generations, Rolls-Royce have held the reputation for doing nothing in haste. Their methods, like their products, have invariably been dignified, refined, civilized and carefully measured—in fact, they have been 'just so'. When it was decided, therefore, to commence the design of a new model to replace the Silver Dawn/R type Bentley series, there was no unseemly rush to get it into production. This, to be sure, is one reason why a new Rolls-Royce is rarely a trend-setter—it might have been up with the current trends when conceived, but would be no more than in the main stream when announced.

Although the Company's staff had been thinking continuously about the improvements and the changes which they would like to make, serious and concentrated drafting of the car did not begin until 1950–51, well over four years before the model was to be put on sale. In the meantime management, who maintained a series of informal contacts between top men (a process which now seems to have been submerged in the much-criticized business of 'product planning'), had been asking itself whether the right type of car was still being made, especially for the increasingly important export markets.

There were, it seems, no serious complaints, and it was not difficult to decide that the new design, different with regard to details, should

The Rolls-Royce Silver Cloud of 1955, which shared its bodyshell and all chassis components with the S series Bentley. The standard steel shell was supplied by the Pressed Steel Co. Ltd

nevertheless follow the same basic layout as before. Of primary importance was the decision to retain the 'traditional' self-supporting rolling chassis, which would lend itself equally to the mounting of standard steel bodywork, or to the careful and leisurely erection of special coachwork in its many forms.

Purely on economic grounds, of course, Rolls-Royce could not seriously consider a unit-construction bodyshell. Apart from the near-impossibility of adaptation for special coachwork (which was still an important if not vital factor when the decision was taken in 1950), there was no escaping the probability that less than twenty thousand examples of the car would be built before it was replaced by another new model.

With those prospects in mind, Rolls-Royce could not justify the cost of unit-construction, and their suppliers, Pressed Steel, prepared to tool up for a new 'standard steel' bodyshell. This concept, incidentally, though new to Rolls-Royce as recently as 1946, had readily been accepted by the clientele. Although it was already becoming clear that the quality of postwar steel left something to be desired, Rolls-Royce saw no reason to retreat from their concept of standardization.

Compared with the existing Silver Dawn/R type model, the new car was to be somewhat larger, with a roomier passenger compartment. It should be no less speedy and certainly no less nimble, but was to take account of modern styling and mechanical trends. There should be provision on the chassis for fittings such as automatic transmission and power-assisted steering, while the body had to make allowances for more comprehensive ventilation systems.

The design had to accommodate a choice of wheelbases (the long-wheelbase models, which had an extra four inches inserted under the passenger cabin, were to follow two years after the original cars), and the basic layout also had to be suitable for a massive stretch to form the basis of a new car planned to replace the Silver Wraith in due course.

The Silver Cloud/S series rolling chassis. The box-section frame, complete with cruciform, the front and the rear suspensions were all new, though similar in layout to the obsolete R type models

Although the general arrangement of the chassis frame and suspension was conventional and recognizably Rolls-Royce, it was almost entirely different in detail. Like the existing model, the new chassis frame had cruciform members under the passenger compartment, was kicked up over the rear axle, and supported the entire running gear; but for the first time it had massive box-section side and cruciform members. It was also significantly bigger in all directions, to allow for a more spacious cabin and style; the wheelbase was up by three inches, the front track by one and a quarter inches and the rear track by two inches.

There were new front and rear suspension layouts. At the front there was what we now see as a conventional coil spring and double wishbone layout in which the upper wishbones also formed links to piston-type dampers, and in which the whole assembly was set in a semi-trailing position. This replaced the Mark V and VI/R

A feature of the Silver Cloud and S series engines was the six-port cylinder head. Compared with the single carburettor Silver Dawn unit, the 4887 cc Silver Cloud was much more powerful though, as usual, no official output figures were ever released. Automatic transmission was standard on all models, as was the friction-type brake servo mounted at the tail of that box

Careful individual assembly of six-cylinder Rolls-Royce/Bentley engines in the workshops at Crewe. The distinctive valve layout (with side exhaust valves) is apparent from the cylinder block seen in the foreground

type/Silver Dawn layout where the top wishbone was semi-leading.

At the rear, the familiar hypoid bevel rear axle was suspended on gaitered half elliptic leaf springs, but to control certain features of roll understeer, to reduce the rear spring wind-up and to help 'balance' the car, there was a new feature. Attached to the right-hand chassis side member and to the axle tube itself was a single radius arm, which because of its shape was universally known as a 'Z bar'. It is interesting to note that Jaguar, in the racing C type introduced at the time the Silver Cloud was being designed, used essentially the same type of axle control. As on the existing model, cam and roller steering allied to a three-piece track rod was chosen, and although the Company was already thinking about the use of power-assisted steering, it was not to be offered at first.

Another familiar Rolls-Royce feature was centralized chassis lubrication, with a mass of metal and flexible piping leading to all those moving joints which would otherwise require greasing. On the front suspension all but the inner wishbone/damper pivots were so treated.

When the car was being designed in the early 1950s, there were no reliable disc brake systems, so Rolls-Royce engineers were faced with the task of stopping a heavier, faster model with smaller drum brakes, as it had been decided to specify 15 inch wheels in place of the 16 inch variety used on the Silver Dawn/R type model. The brake drums themselves were reduced in diameter to 11·25 inch, but given 3·0 inch widths, which resulted in a 22 per cent increase in lining area. Front brakes now had twin trailing shoes, and the combination of hydraulic front and hydro-mechanical rear brakes had power-assistance from the familiar, complex, but extremely effective mechanical friction-type servo fitted to a cross-shaft at the tail of the gearbox. This device, originally invented by Hispano-Suiza and fitted to all Rolls-Royce cars built after 1925, acted like a friction clutch when the brake pedal was depressed, and its original tendency to 'lag' somewhat was greatly minimized for this, its final application.

The engine as well as the chassis, was greatly improved and changed. All models, right from the start, were to be equipped with the 4887 cc engine size which the public would see introduced on the last series of R type Continental Bentleys, but there would be an entirely new light-alloy cylin-

Except for the bonnet top panels, there was absolutely no 'sheet metal' difference between the Silver Cloud and S series models, but no one could mistake the radiator grille treatments

der head, and for the first time the 'standard steel' Rolls-Royce and Bentleys would have precisely the same engine tune. In fact, this presaged a major improvement in performance for the Rolls-Royce, for the current Silver Dawn was equipped with a single (Zenith) carburettor 4556 cc engine and could barely reach 90 mph.

Although the new cylinder head retained the distinctive F-head layout, with a large overhead inlet valve and a side-mounted exhaust valve, it was to have individual inlet and exhaust ports for the first time. Other changes included the use of full-length cylinder liners, a crankshaft with integral balance weights and a front-mounted vibration damper. Originally, engines for the standard cars were given cylinder heads with a compression ratio of 6·6:1, though those for use in Bentley Continentals had slightly different heads, with a ratio of 7·25:1. As usual, Rolls-Royce were much more interested in the ultimate in refinement, smooth torque delivery and silent and silky operation, so no attempt was made to boost the power to unacceptable levels at the expense of flexibility. As ever, peak power figures were not revealed, but a study of that historic I. Mech. E. paper (*The History of a Dimension*), read by Harry Grylls to the Automobile Division in 1963, suggests that something like 150 bhp at 4000 rpm might have been near the truth. Original 4¼-litre B60 engines built for the Mark VI Bentley in 1946 had produced 132 bhp at 4000 rpm.

Behind the engines, which differed externally between models only by the identification on their cylinder head covers, it was decided to standardize the General Motors Hydra-Matic (soon to be written into the language as Hydramatic) transmission, which was completely automatic, providing four forward speeds in conjunction with a fluid coupling between engine and gearbox proper. This had been offered as an option on the existing models from 1952, and was standardized on the Silver Dawn in 1953, and on the R type Bentley in 1954, although the well-developed four-speed synchromesh gearbox, complete with its right hand change, continued to be available at no extra cost. Rolls-Royce were so impressed by this modern North American component that their only important modification was to have the rear modified to accept the cross-shaft drive to their friction-driven brake servo.

Above *This is a left-hand-drive Silver Cloud, complete with sumptuously equipped standard steel bodyshell. In those days, one definitely did not step down into a car of this character and breeding*

Left *This is the facia of a long-wheelbase Silver Cloud I, complete with division. As on all such cars, the automatic transmission control is on the steering column. The T-handle on the right is for operation of the hand brake*

Silver Clouds and S series models had massive but graceful lines, as instanced by this Series I model. Compared with the obsolete R type, there was only a little more passenger accommodation, but a considerably larger boot

Although management was entirely happy to make the automatic transmission virtually mandatory on their standard saloons and most of the chassis supplied for the fitment of special coachwork, they realised that a proportion of customers for the Bentley Continentals, even if rather more mature and less sporting than the type of person who bought a super-sports or GT car, might still want manual transmission. It was decided to offer this as an option (but *not* as standard equipment) on the new series of Continentals. As we shall see in the next chapter, the option proved increasingly hard to get, and when existing new-car stocks ran out in 1957, the choice was withdrawn.

Although the design and layout of the chassis was of great interest, it was the bodywork which drew the most attention. As with the existing standard models, Rolls-Royce decided to place the order for their 'standard steel' saloon coachwork with the Pressed Steel Company at Cowley; although Rolls-Royce had no resident inspectors at that plant, and in spite of the fact that some

Conversion from normal to long wheelbase was so skilfully done that one had to look hard for the differences. This Silver Cloud lwb model, with division, has larger rear doors and no quarter windows within the frames, while there is a separate quarter window behind the door and over the top of the wheel arch cut out. Two-tone paintwork helps give the impression of a long and very sleek car.

tooling was not nearly as permanent or complex as it might have been for a mass-production shell, the quality of the shells was an improvement on what had gone before. With the exception of the door pressings and the bonnet and boot lid panels (which were light-alloy), all other pressings were in steel. Principal assembly was at Cowley with final assembly, preparation, corrosion-protection and the customary painstaking painting processes carried out at the Crewe factory.

Apart from the use of different radiator shells (even the patrician Rolls-Royce proboscis in that noble Grecian style had not been other than a 'fake' since the late 1930s), there was no mechanical or basic body difference between the two marques. It is worth noting that one had to pay £90 extra (basic) for the pleasure of choosing Rolls-Royce instead of Bentley.

The body style itself, by Rolls-Royce themselves (though it seems certain that they took discreet advice and soundings from one or two of their favourite coachbuilders, particularly H. J. Mul-

Which radiator style is the most impressive on a 1950s' Crewe product—the rounded Bentley style, or the angular Rolls-Royce style?

liner and Park Ward), was massive, roomy, well-proportioned and altogether what one had come to expect from the makers of 'The Best Car in the World'. Compared with the Silver Dawn/R type Bentley series, the new car had a radically raised front wing crown line which swept gracefully across front and rear doors. The rear wing line, as before, effectively began on the skin of the rear door, also had a raised and more pronounced crown line. On the one hand this ensured that the distance between the doors could be greater (for increased body width), and the stowage accommodation in the boot could be vastly increased, but on the other it meant that access to the engine compartment was rather less convenient. On the basis that (according to the well-founded legend) 'Rolls-Royce cars do not break', and that they would be maintained by mechanics who were paid not to complain about these things, this drawback was accepted without demur.

There was a significant increase in glass area

Far right *Outside it is dark, and drizzling, but the Rolls-Royce owner must have felt very secure as he looked out over the Silver Cloud's long bonnet*

This Silver Cloud drophead coupé is one of a limited number of cars built by H. J. Mulliner, which was in fact a two-door conversion of the standard steel saloon bodyshell, and retains the same basic wing and body lines . . .

compared with the existing bodyshell, not only due to rather larger apertures, but also to the fact that the new design of shell used what are known as 'half frame' doors, instead of door pressings which completely envelop the glass. Without making the door apertures themselves vastly larger, there was more available light above their waistlines.

As before, the nose of the cars was also distinguished by two extra driving lamps above the bumper, which had those distinctive over-riders quite unlike anything else at the time. There was a radio aerial mounted on the roof just behind the screen.

Although the whole car was a mere eight inches longer than before, and nearly five inches wider, not all this extra bulk had been allocated to the passengers. The Silver Cloud was only three inches wider across the rear seat than the Silver Dawn had been, there were perhaps two inches

. . . and looks very smart, in Bentley form, with the hood folded away. Inevitably, there was less space in the rear seats than in the standard steel saloon

more across the front seats, and no more leg room at all for the rear seat passengers. For all that, the footwells did not narrow as sharply as on the R type body, and it was only the exceptional plushy and sumptuous seats which stopped the new car's interior from feeling altogether more spacious.

Apart from the fine finish of the paintwork and the exterior ornamentation, it was the internal equipment, the fittings, the seats and the carpets which made the new car such a demonstrably upper-class creation. There was nothing to curtail front seat lounging space, and though this had a bench seat cushion, it had large individual back rests which could be adjusted for rake independently of each other. Glossy, beautifully finished picnic tables were, of course, let in to the back of these seats. The rear seat, too, was beautifully trimmed and finished, with a big fold-down centre arm-rest, and vanity mirrors in each rear quarter which included stowage space for

cosmetics. Genuine wood cappings were fitted to the door rails, and every piece of wood matched the material of the main facia panel; the exact piece of wood chosen was noted during initial assembly, and spare material was kept to one side in case an owner should ever damage his car and need replacement fittings.

The walnut facia was neat, comprehensive and under-stated, and included a built-in radio (which was not at all commonplace in Europe at this

Even by the mid-1950s, H. J. Mulliner was beginning to develop coachbuilt styles with much more pronounced 'straight through' body lines. This Bentley style should be compared with the Mulliner drop-head convertible on pages 28 and 29

time). The automatic gearchange was on the steering column, while those rare Continentals with manual transmission were to have a right-hand change unless left-hand drive when it went to the column. It was intended to provide ride-control of rear suspension damper settings, which on the car was electrically selected from a switch on the steering column.

There was a particularly complex and effective ventilation system of which the engineers were very proud. For the first time in the world of motoring, it offered separate systems for demisting and heating; thus a customer could enjoy cool air around his face and warm air round his feet. There were two heat exchanger units, one on each side of the engine bay, which drew fresh air from inlets set low down in the nose at each side of the radiator grille; the right side served the windscreen, while the left side served the passenger toeboard and fed ducting leading to outlets on the propeller shaft tunnel facing the rear seats. At 80 mph the combined output was as much as 11 kW—the equivalent of an 11-bar electric fire.

Even though design and development of the new car was a major undertaking for Rolls-Royce, the 250-strong engineering team was at least not hampered by safety, emission or other nationalistic legislation. As it was also possible for many components, and ideas, to be tested on 'slave' cars in the department, which looked outwardly like normal R types or Silver Dawns, only five true prototypes were built at Crewe before Pressed Steel were ready to deliver the first completely 'off-tools' S type bodyshell.

By the beginning of 1955, after more than four years' concentrated development and tooling work, Rolls-Royce were ready to put the new S series cars into production at Crewe. Even though almost everything about the new cars *was* new, and though building of the last Silver Dawns and R type Bentleys was to go on full-blast until May 1955, there was virtually no hiatus between the two. The new models were announced together, in the last week of April 1955, and deliveries began the following month.

Now, with a projected ten year life ahead of them, the cars' prospects were being put on the line. Would they sell? Were they what the customers really wanted?

Chapter 3
Bentley Continental

Unfortunately for Bentley enthusiasts this is to be rather a short section as, by comparison with the luscious R type Continentals built from 1952 to 1955, S type models became progressively less special. Apart from the brief period in 1956–1957 when Continentals were the only Crewe products with 8·0:1 compression ratio engines, they had virtually identical engines to the standard steel saloons. Once the new vee-8 engine was standardized in the autumn of 1959, Continentals were really only distinguished by their special coachwork, and their performance was close to that of the standard steel saloons.

However, as with the previous models, Rolls-Royce always intended that the Bentley Continentals should be rather distinctive, and that they should all be clothed in graceful two-door coachwork. The time taken to build such bodies, carefully and in no great haste by skilled craftsmen, explains why the first S type Continental was not delivered before the end of September 1955, even though its rolling chassis had been produced in March of that year.

In effect, the R type Continental had been created by H. J. Mulliner, so it was quite reasonable that this concern had produced all but fifteen of the original 208 R type cars. For the new model, however, Rolls-Royce decreed that Mulliner should share the business with their

This Bentley Continental SI Sports Saloon with coachwork by H. J. Mulliner features what appear to be slightly less pronounced rear wings and no wheel spats

Right *The comprehensively equipped facia of a series I Continental, complete with a rev-counter, on the far right of the instrument panel*

'Flying Spur' was the title given to this rather rounded four-door sports saloon style by H. J. Mulliner on the Bentley Continental SI chassis. It first appeared on 1958 models

subsidiary Park Ward, who each produced about the same number of six-cylinder cars built between 1955 and 1959. As with the R types, there were coupés and convertibles, though no four-door derivatives at first.

Compared with the original S type chassis the chassis used for the fitment of Continental coachwork differed in several significant details. As one might expect, the overall gearing was considerably higher (to take account of a better aerodynamic shape, and more powerful engines), with a final drive ratio of 2·923:1 compared with 3·42:1 for the standard steel models. The Continental engine, complete with the individual inlet and exhaust ports of the latest design, also had a 7·25:1 compression ratio.

Above *Under the skin is the 1956 Bentley Continental chassis, and this is a drophead coupé body style by Park Ward. The total price, when new in 1955; £6766*

Right *Probably the very first Rolls-Royce or Bentley to have completely 'straight-through' wing lines was this SII coachbuilt model, from Park Ward, which appeared in drophead coupé or fixed-head coupé two-door styles*

The most important feature of the Continental, however, was that—at first, at least—it could be supplied with the old-type close-ratio synchromesh manual gearbox to order, even though automatic transmission had now been standardized (except for a very few cars) on all other derivatives of the new design. Even so, Rolls-Royce only continued to offer this option with great reluctance. Very few SI Continentals were so equipped, and the option was withdrawn by the spring of 1957.

Power-assisted steering was optional at first but was standardized in 1958, and records show that fifty cars already at the coachbuilders were converted to power steering after that announcement had been made—at considerable expense!

Performance of the original cars was disappointingly close to that of the standard steel models, so from the autumn of 1956 the compression ratio of the 4887 cc engines was raised from 7·25:1 to 8·0:1. A more important change, perhaps, was the adoption of larger inlet valves plus 2-inch SU carburettors, which raised the

James Young's interpretation of a four-door 'Flying Spur' style on the Continental chassis was very similar to that of H. J. Mulliner, but subtly different, particularly around the rear of the passenger cabin

H. J. Mulliner built a whole series of impressive two-door styles on the Bentley Continental chassis, this one being on the basis of a vee-8 engined SII model

peak horsepower by no less than thirteen per cent. For more than a year, until this engine was adopted for all other Silver Cloud derivatives, it made the Continental significantly quicker than any of its stablemates. Road tests by magazines as meticulous as *The Autocar* demonstrated maximum speeds of nearly 120 mph, and the ability to sprint majestically up to 100 mph from rest in about 40 seconds—marginally slower than that of the original R type Continentals. One must admit though that the later cars had rather bulkier, less wind-cheating and undoubtedly heavier chassis and body components.

From the autumn of 1957, H. J. Mulliner

This series III four-door saloon style by James Young is a development of that company's 'Flying Spur' design of the late 1950s. The false number plate tells us that this, in fact, is a 1963 model

Except that it has slant-styled quadruple headlamps, and other detail changes, this is the same basic Mulliner-Park Ward 'straight-through' style as the series II drophead coupé already depicted on page 36 . . .

introduced a new and very sleek four-door saloon style on the Continental chassis which they dubbed the 'Flying Spur'. Although Mulliner wanted to call this a Continental model, Rolls-Royce resisted on the grounds that they had always intended 'Continentals' to be entities involving low wind resistance, lightness and high performance. Mulliner, however, kept on reiterating that their Flying Spur satisfied all these requirements, and after it also became clear that their customers had begun to consider the Flying Spurs as 'Continentals', the Company gave in with good grace. The Flying Spur is the near-unique example of four-door coachwork on the Continental chassis, although a few similar examples were later constructed by James Young.

This, however, was the high point for the Continental, for when the SII model was brought in during the autumn of 1959, there was no special high-performance version of the new vee-8 engine. Overall gearing of the SII Continental was not changed (although that of the standard steel cars had been raised substantially), and the cars

... and this is how that drophead coupé style had evolved in the same period

were neither faster nor more economical than the standard type. Their prices, however, were still very distinctive; a 1960-model standard steel car's basic price was £3995, while that of a Mulliner Continental was no less than £5730. Both prices were to be raised in May 1960, and (in the case of Continentals only) again in February 1961.

In the autumn of 1962, SII models gave way to their final developments, the SIII cars, at which point the Continental chassis became almost indistinguishable from the standard chassis, except for its slighter smaller-section tyres. Bodies, whether four-door, two-door, or two-door convertible, continued to be striking and distinctive. Those produced by Park Ward, which finally ushered in the era of the 'straight through' wing line along the side of these patrician cars, were introduced in the autumn of 1959, and graced the line until it was withdrawn at the beginning of 1966. Although these SII and SIII Continentals were always lofty and massive compared with the Silver Shadows which were shortly to follow, there seems to be no doubt that their styling was a direct influence on the later quantity-production car.

As production of separate-chassis S type Bentleys drew to a close in 1965, it spelt the end of the road for the famous and legendary name of 'Continental'. The last chassis was delivered to its coachbuilder on 29 November, three months after the last SIII saloon had been delivered, and it did not actually reach its customer until the end of January 1966.

For the record, there were 431 SI Continentals, 388 SII Continentals, and 312 of the final SIII variety. H. J. Mulliner was credited with building 507 of the bodies, Park Ward with 458, and the combined M-PW concern accounted for seventy-five more. Only three other coachbuilders added to the total; James Young, who built eighty-one examples, being the most significant.

Statistically, we can see that S type Continental production was only fifteen per cent of the Bentley total. This, and the fact that the chassis specification had progressively been standardized over the years, meant that Rolls-Royce saw no justification for continuing the Continental name into the new types of Silver Shadows and Bentley T series cars which were introduced at the end of 1965.

For all that, many enthusiasts look upon the latter-day Bentley Corniche models (which *are* faster and carry special coachwork) as 'Continentals', and there is a groundswell of opinion which suggests that the exclusive Rolls-Royce Camargues of 1975 to date should definitely have been radiator'd and badged as Bentley Continentals. From time to time, it is true, the Company has talked wistfully of reintroducing something special with a Bentley identity. How much longer must the true enthusiast wait?

Chapter 4
Design Revolution–the new V8 engine

Throughout the 1940s and 1950s many people took a cynical approach and felt that Rolls-Royce was still living in the past. Their cars and their attitudes to motoring, it was said, were entrenched in a bygone age. If demand for their cars *had* slumped, or such splendid machines as the Bentley Continentals had not been produced, I might have been prepared to listen, but I would never have agreed with their view. To me, it was obvious that one very important branch of the Company—the design engineering group—was looking to its future.

Starting from the first design, made in 1946, one of the most important projects being developed behind closed doors at Crewe was that of an entirely new engine for use in future models—the first new unit, incidentally, since the design of the Phantom III's vee-12 engine at the beginning of the 1930s. It was needed for two reasons, one being that the existing six-cylinder engine had finally reached the end of its useful development life, and the other being that much more power was likely to be needed in the Company's cars for the 1960s, 1970s and beyond. A new engine had to be designed with a long production run in view—not only was it usual for Rolls-Royce to use the same well-proven engine layout for a long time, but it made a great deal of economic sense.

The immediately obvious alternative of using further-developed B80 straight-eight units (as fitted to the Phantom IV, and to a whole variety of military machines) was discarded almost at once. Not only was the B80 too large (too long *and* too heavy), but its crankshaft could not satisfactorily be controlled at the higher revolutions it might be asked to attain in—say—a latter-day Continental, and it was moreover, impossible to stretch any further.

Design of an all-new unit, began in the early 1950s; it was soon decided to go for a vee-8 layout. Historically speaking, Rolls-Royce had links with vee-12 engines (not only with the Phantom III engine, but with the phenomenally successful Merlin aero-engine and its derivatives. Even by their exalted standards, however, this was thought likely to be costly, complex, and heavy. The vee-8 layout had so many potential attractions which included compactness, relatively light weight, and eminent suitability for use with automatic transmission, that it had no real rivals. It is intriguing to recall that Jaguar, when faced with a similar choice in the 1960s, plumped for the vee-12 solution and later cancelled a vee-8 derivative of that engine! One might also mention in passing that there had only previously been one other automotive Rolls-Royce vee-8 engine—of which only a handful were made in 1905–1906.

For Rolls-Royce the new design, which was running at the experimental stage and installed in cars even before the six-cylinder Silver Cloud was announced in 1955, was a resourceful and far-sighted leap into the future. The age-old six-cylinder engine had used a cast-iron cylinder block, whereas the new unit used a light-alloy casting. The B60 family relied on an F-head valve gear layout, with overhead inlet and side exhaust valves, whereas the vee-8 had a conventional overhead valve scheme with in line valves. The six-cylinder engine, even in its final stages, had been 'undersquare' by contrast with the eight's significantly 'oversquare' dimensions. The six-cylinder engine had used dry cylinder liners, while the vee-8 had used wet liners. The basic and unquestioned success of the new engine can, however, be summed up in one sentence—it was 10 lb lighter, 27·5 per cent larger in capacity, and probably produced 20/25 bhp more peak horsepower.

Although the engine bay of the Silver Cloud was not specifically laid out with the new engine in mind, it had always been thought that a vee-formation engine would eventually be needed, so it was not surprising that the new unit should eventually drop into the space with the minimum

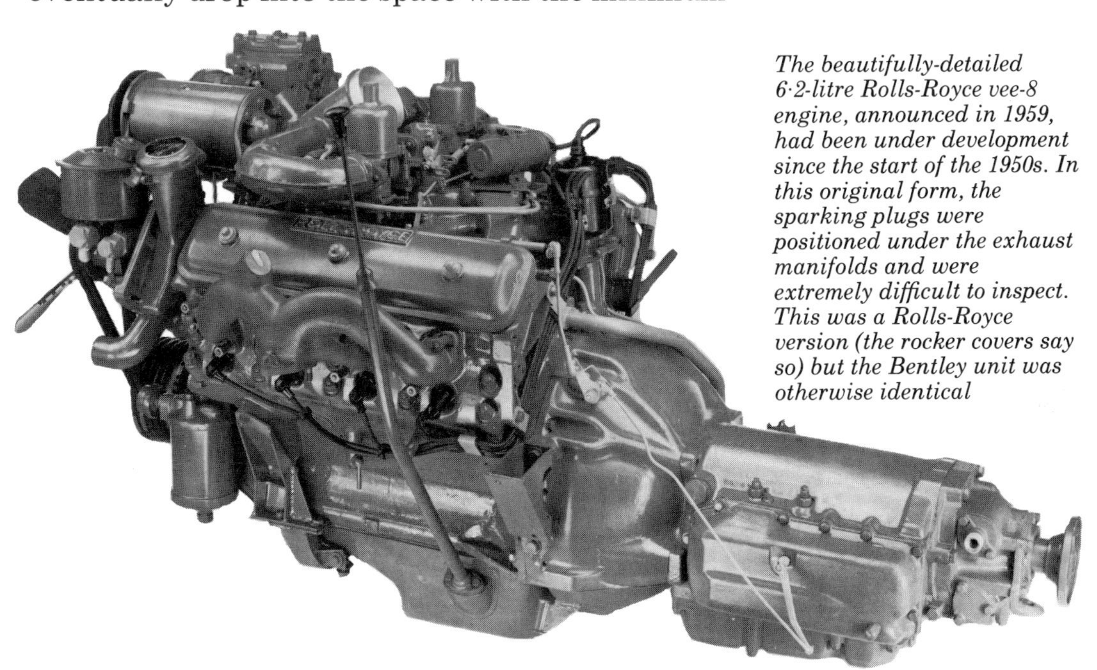

The beautifully-detailed 6·2-litre Rolls-Royce vee-8 engine, announced in 1959, had been under development since the start of the 1950s. In this original form, the sparking plugs were positioned under the exhaust manifolds and were extremely difficult to inspect. This was a Rolls-Royce version (the rocker covers say so) but the Bentley unit was otherwise identical

of aggravation to designers and production staff alike. However, to minimize the engine's width as much as possible, the lines of valves were effectively made to lean inwards towards the centre of the unit at twenty-eight degrees from the cylinder centre lines, and the carburettors and inlet manifolds were of course on top of the engine, in the centre of the cylinder 'vee'.

When design commenced and when the first engines were built, the vee-8's engine size was 5·2

Apart from the new vee-8 engine, there were many other detail differences between the rolling chassis of the 1959 series II and the 1955 series I models. The location of the rear axle 'Z bar' is particularly clear in this illustration

litres, which endowed it with approximately the same maximum power output as the 4·9-litre 'six', but with rather more torque.

Well before the decision about the engine's final production specification had to be taken, the need for more vehicle performance and hence a larger power output became clear, especially as there was no slackening off in the tendency for production *and* coachbuilt bodies to become progressively heavier. The engine's swept volume was therefore increased to no less than 6·2 litres—by nearly twenty per cent—and the actual detail dimensions of 104·1 × 91·4 mm (4·10 × 3·60 in) bore and stroke, and the capacity of 6230 cc, were then to remain unchanged from the introduction of the engine through to 1970.

Although the Company's engineers readily admit that they studied examples of several of their rivals' modern vee-8 engine designs (contemporary North American developments were regarded as especially significant), there seems to be no evidence at all of any direct copying. By the standards of the day the new Rolls-Royce vee-8 engine design was compact and conventional, and apart from its use of light-alloy cylinder block and heads, it was mainly distinguished by the use of hydraulic tappets, bought in complete from Chrysler of Detroit.

Right from the start it was clear to most observers with technical training that it was an engine which was initially (and intentionally) being produced in 'Mark I' form, at the start of a planned long life, as that doyen of British technical writers, *The Autocar*'s Harry Mundy, pointed out in his analysis of the design on its announcement in 1959: '. . . it is obvious that the engine is deliberately restricted on the carburettor side, leaving plenty of development in hand when the need arises to increase performance'.

By 1963, the model had progressed to become series III, and the engine was more powerful than before, but in almost all other details there is little obvious change. The height of the radiator shells—Rolls Royce or Bentley—had been reduced to accord with slightly revised styling

And so it was. Although the detail of the engine looked deceptively simple—which was due as much to the need to keep costs to reasonable limits, and to ease the machining problems, as it was to satisfy its designers' conservatism—the main stress-carrying members (block, heads, crankshaft and other moving parts) were quite clearly at ease with their original tasks. Indeed, almost any other firm but Rolls-Royce would surely have been tempted to prove the worth of their excellent new design by encouraging its use in some sort of racing car. (There was even a strong suggestion that this would be done later in the 1960s, but it all came most intriguingly to nothing).

Indeed, from the new vee-8 engine's announcement in September 1959 to date, no maximum power or torque figure has ever been revealed. Like Aston Martin, who are not in the same type of market, but are equally committed to making excellent vee-8 engines without having to stoop to distorted claims, Rolls-Royce prefer to keep their own counsel regarding acceptable standards and to let their cars' performance and economy speak for itself. That age-old answer of 'sufficient' has always been enough.

During the life of the engine in the Silver Cloud family, no major changes were to be made to the engine, though with the introduction of the SIII derivatives in the autumn of 1962 it was stated that a power increase of seven per cent had been provided by means of higher compression ratio cylinder heads (9·0:1 instead of 8·0:1) and the use of larger choked SU carburettors (2·0 inch in place of the original 1·75 inch instruments). We might hazard a guess, therefore, that the Cloud and SIII models had engines producing about 215/220 bhp.

In the last decade, however, since the latest Silver Shadow range has proliferated, there has been a constant battle between strangulation by exhaust emission legislation and the need to maintain or even improve vehicle performance. When the Corniche was revealed in 1971 (effectively a latter-day Continental), it was admitted that ten per cent more power had been liberated, though it was always said that the 6·75-litre engine which had arrived during the previous year had done no more than repel the detuning needed to meet USA emission requirements. One way or another, it seems that 1980's vee-8 engine may be only marginally more powerful than the 1959 variety, though it should be more flexible, possessed of somewhat more torque, and altogether cleaner in terms of its exhaust gases.

Vee-8 engines on test at Crewe before being fitted to new cars. Each and every unit was checked in this way before being approved for assembly into a chassis

Although the engine was very straightforward and conventional by contemporary vee-8 standards, it followed the expected Rolls-Royce standards by being beautifully made, exquisitely finished and presented, and as unobtrusively efficient as one could expect. A snap opening of the throttle produced none of the thrash and commotion expected from a high-performance North American engine, but a rather busier murmur and a subdued sense of increased purpose, all of which resulted in a smart increase in acceleration. It was never necessary to raise one's voice or to turn up the radio merely because one was choosing to cruise at much higher speeds.

Because most of the major castings were in aluminium alloy (a notoriously efficient transmitter of sound), and nothing more elaborate than twin SU carburettors of conventional design were used, this discreet behaviour was all the more remarkable, and was a great tribute to Rolls-

Royce's air-cleaning and sound insulating methods as well as to the diligence of the engineers at Crewe in achieving this high standard.

Although a Rolls-Royce owner was not reckoned to spend much of his time looking at or working on his vee-8 engine, it was presented to him with great attention to detail and style. Forgings, castings and connections were fashioned, located, and inter-related with some care. To locate and fasten the heads to the block not two, but four rows of holding-down studs were employed. Wherever components might be on view, they were not left in their raw, or even machined state. Invariably they were coated—often painted—in some suitable finish. And yet for all that, the engine was not laid out for easy attention and maintenance. To gain access to the carburation, the air-cleaner had to be released and swivelled out of the way. Worse, access to the spark plugs (which were located in the side of the cylinder heads, underneath the exhaust manifolds) was almost impossible from above, and special access panels in the inner wheel arches had to be provided to ease the problem.

One way in which Rolls-Royce ensured that their new power unit would not need constant attention and improvement was by refusing to countenance the use of a chain to drive the camshaft, mounted in the centre of the 'vee'. Like the six-cylinder engine which it replaced, the vee-8's camshaft was driven by helical-toothed spur gears, which not only ensured perfect and constant timing but were quieter in operation than chains, and would not grow slack and badly worn in middle age; even the massive camshaft gear was of aluminium alloy, and was given a series of corrugations in its section so that vibrations would be reduced to an acceptable minimum. In an entirely logical way of which both Sir Henry

Royce and (latterly) that genius in engine design, Keith Duckworth, would have approved, the ignition distributor was driven from the tail of the crankshaft, adjacent to the flywheel, where the timing was most likely to approximate to ideal requirements.

It goes without saying that machining and assembly of these massive and refined engines was a lengthy, leisurely and almost infinitely careful business. Whereas a modern mass-produced engine might receive the most cursory motoring over under artificial conditions to make sure that it is, at least, completely assembled, the engine of a Rolls-Royce is invariably run in most carefully, set up and tuned, power tested, and only released for fitment to a car if its performance falls within a very narrow band of acceptability.

A look at the performance achieved—in miles per hour, miles per gallon, in seconds, and in average speeds—tells its own story as far as the vee-8 engine and the Silver Cloud family was concerned. Compared with the original six-cylinder engined model, a SII has a maximum speed higher by at least 15 mph, a cut of something like one third in the time needed to accelerate to any speed from rest, and virtually no penalty in day-to-day operating economy, in spite of the fact that the car's weight had risen by around 350 lb. And these, mark you, are not claims put about by the Public Relations department at Crewe, but were recorded by the influential motoring magazines, *Autocar* and *Motor*.

It confirms that the work expended at Crewe over such a period of time was all worth it, and if only we had known, gave promise of even more exciting Rolls-Royce performances in the future. In every way, therefore, the vee-8 engine has been a 'building block' vital to the Company's well-being and its long-term prospects.

Chapter 5
Ten years of evolution, 1955-1965

By the time the new models were announced, Rolls-Royce's car-making reputation was such that they could almost be guaranteed a fulsome reception. National newspaper headlines, as expected, were positively euphoric, and even the motoring magazines were enthusiastic. *The Motor*, for instance, commented that, '. . . although they are not the largest, the fastest or the most glamorous cars available, they are probably the finest examples obtainable anywhere in the world . . ..' *The Autocar*, too, were very deferential: 'With the reputation for making the finest car in the world, it is no easy task to introduce a new range of cars that will be better than the models they superseded, but cost very little more. Yet with the introduction of the new Rolls-Royce Silver Cloud and the Bentley series S this is just what has been done . . . No part of the car can be analysed in detail without bringing to light a most interesting development story, and there is little doubt that these fine new cars will carry on the makers' tradition and reputation.'

Among the potential customers and those dealers lucky enough to be charged with selling the cars, the new models were very well received, if only because those people had become so very accustomed to looking at the smart though basically pre-war style of the Silver Dawns and R types. Almost at once, however, it became clear that there had been a fundamental shift in demand. Production of Bentley Continentals was virtually limited to the number of bodies which could be constructed by H. J. Mulliner and by Park Ward, but the considerable boost given to the performance of the Rolls-Royce derivative (compared with the single-carburettor Silver Dawn) had worked wonders for its prospects; it is worth pointing out, in fact, that this was the very first Rolls-Royce motor car which could reach a genuine 100 mph maximum speed.

Whereas with the previous model range the vast majority of standard steel cars had always been Bentleys, Silver Clouds and S series Bentleys were built in almost the same numbers. As the years went by, and the price differential remained virtually the same, the balance tipped even further in favour of the Rolls-Royce derivative; in the last three years, over sixty per cent of all standard steel SIIIs would carry the exquisite Rolls-Royce radiator. (It is interesting to note that following the introduction of the monocoque Silver Shadow in 1965, this trend became even more pronounced). Let no one, however, think that these fine new cars were being assembled with unseemly haste. In the first four years of production (before the new vee-8 engine was announced) no more than twenty-five standard steel saloons were delivered in an average week, and it is worth noting that at the same time not more than two coachbuilt Bentley Continentals would leave the London-based coachbuilding concerns. This leisurely rate of production makes it all the more remarkable that Pressed Steel, for instance, found it worth making such a limited supply of components.

Above *The chassis assembly line at Crewe (the cars have six-cylinder engines, and are therefore SI types) is busy, but the process was never to be hurried. At this point assembly was almost complete, and finished examples are parked behind the row of work benches*

Right *Painting a new bodyshell. This is destined to be a Bentley S series model—the clue is in the rounded profile of the bonnet top panels*

Left *The point every visitor wishes to see, where the bodyshell meets its chassis for the first time. Great care was needed at this juncture, so that the ultimate in refinement could be guaranteed on completion*

Above *Coachlining the finished paintwork of an S series Bentley, a task needing considerable artistry and a steady hand. Could one tackle this sort of job with a hangover?*

Left *Every car—this was a left-hand-drive Silver Cloud destined, probably, for North America—was given a lengthy and detailed road test before being passed off. The bumper coverings were to give protection from bumps and scrapes in transit*

YLG 990

Above *Both the machines in the picture are Rolls-Royce powered, the Silver Cloud I by a six-cylinder 4·9-litre piston engine, and the Comet 4 aircraft by four Rolls-Royce turbojets*

Far left *From this angle, no one could fail to identify a Rolls-Royce. In fact it is a series I model, in long-wheelbase form, with a division, the sort of car one expected to be driven by a chauffeur*

Once established, however, the Silver Cloud family was not allowed to languish unimproved, or to sell on its own merits. Well before the car was first released (but not yet *au point* in 1955), a power-assisted steering system was under development, and this duly made its bow just a year after the new model's launch.

At first available for export only (but on home-market models from the autumn of 1956), the power-assistance involved a Hobourn-Eaton engine-driven hydraulic pump, and a Rolls-Royce control-valve assembly in tandem with the normal Marles steering box. Movement of the steering-wheel fed oil under pressure to an actuating cylinder mounted on the front suspen-

The long-wheelbase Silver Cloud I, complete with chauffeur, who was not even available as an extra, outside their owner's (and employer's) home

sion cross-member, whose ram was fixed to an idler lever in the steering linkage. In the context of the well-filled, if not over-crowded engine bay and front end, this was a neat and unobtrusive installation. It was also arranged in such a way that if, unthinkably, the power-assistance failed, then the steering reverted to normal manual operation, albeit at higher-than-normal efforts, and with a little backlash which the driver could just feel. Maximum effort at the steering-wheel, in parking situations, was no more than 12 lb.

At the same time (with introduction for home market cars also delayed until the autumn of 1956), a complex air-conditioning system, which allowed the car's interior to be comprehensively cooled, was also made available. This installation did not take the place of the standard ventilation system, which was only capable of heating the interior, or of passing air at ambient temperature through its ducting. For that reason, and as the basic cost was no less than £385 (or £577 with British purchase tax), ten per cent of the basic price of the complete car, demand even among affluent Rolls-Royce and Bentley customers was somewhat restricted. This compares interestingly with the great success of the power-assisted steering option, which cost a mere £110 basic, and was very popular in all markets.

Like the hydraulic pump of the power-assisted steering installation, the compressor for the air-conditioning was driven from the front of the engine, which was beginning to look like a veritable cat's cradle of belting, bracketry and fittings. The major components in the system including the actual refrigeration unit were located in the boot, immediately behind the rear seat squab, and the condensing radiator which

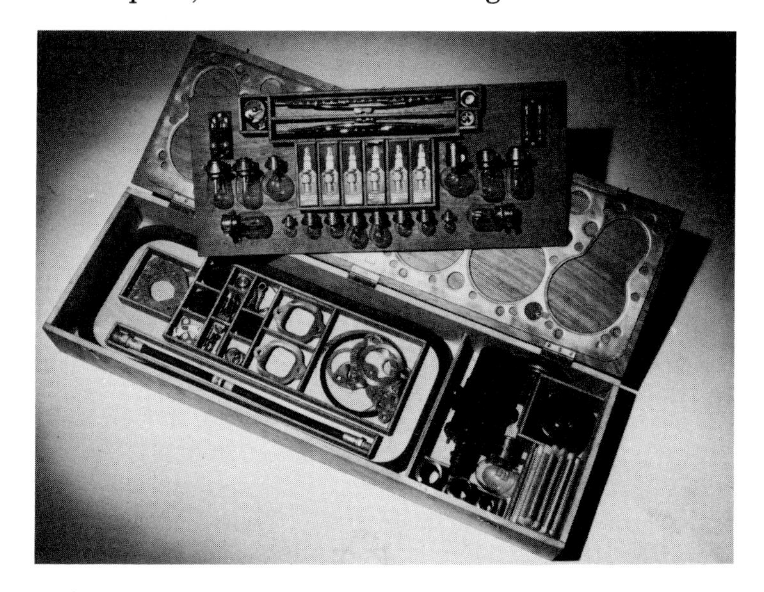

Even when it came to the supply and packaging of a Continental Touring Kit, Rolls-Royce went to considerable pains to get the equipment and the layout absolutely right. The six sparking plugs tell us that this was for a series I model, and of course the cylinder head gasket is quite unmistakable

Above *This view of a series II Silver Cloud long-wheelbase model shows that most of the extra space was allocated to the rear seat passengers*

Right *Some of the extra space in a long-wheelbase model, compared with the 'standard steel' bodyshell, was lost to the division, which incorporated the walnut picnic tables normally found in the back of the front seats, and a central cocktail cabinet*

was mounted immediately in front of the engine cooling radiator.

The system operated on the recirculating air principle. Air from the car's interior was drawn into the unit through a grille on the rear parcel shelf and, after cooling in the 400 cu ft per minute capacity unit, was ducted back into the car through slots built into the trim panels behind and above the rear doors. This capacity, incidentally, was claimed to be the equivalent of fifty ordinary domestic-style house refrigerators, and promised a complete change of air in about one and a half minutes.

It was a measure of the Company's attention to detail that they raised the recommended engine idling speed of cars fitted with this system so that (where legally allowed) the car could be left to

When the Silver Cloud's body was being styled, no detail was neglected. Every component—taillamps, bumper overriders, boot lid handle and badging—was carefully considered. Only the bumper badge identifies the derivative from the rear of the car

Once mechanically complete, this SII Bentley received a lot of careful 'spit and polish' to make sure that any minor imperfections and blemishes were removed. Nothing it seems was too much trouble at Rolls-Royce

idle, unattended, with the interior still cool on the driver's return!

The refrigeration system could also be supplied for coachbuilt cars, but was considerably more expensive (£550 basic, £825 with British purchase tax) due to the extra individual fittings required.

A year after these two important features had been made available, and at the same time as the Flying Spur made headlines, a long-wheelbase version of the standard steel saloons was phased in, offered as either Rolls-Royce or Bentley, and came complete with an electrically operated glass division between front and rear seats. This variation on the theme had a body shell based on that of the standard steel saloon, but was comprehensively modified by Park Ward at Willesden.

The wheelbase was increased by four inches—from 10 ft 3 in to 10 ft 7 in—which meant that a special new chassis frame was required from John Thompson Motor Pressings. The extra length was allocated to improving the lot of the rear seat

Standard four door Bentley S1. Few 'production' cars have such a handsome line when photographed as three-quarters rear.

Above *Bentley's SI Continental with body by H. J. Mulliner*

Right *Silver Cloud SCII still looks the part even in all white*

Far Right *Ex Duke of Norfolk Bentley SII lwb by James Young*

682 PPO

This well kept SCII appears immaculate even under the bonnet. Although the V8 engine fits the engine bay well, there is not all that much room for the mechanic's hands

Connolly leather and Wilton carpet, walnut veneer and the best of British steel – the same Silver Cloud II's interior

Left *From the side there is not much to distinguish this as a Silver Cloud III*

Below *However, this could only be an SCIII lwb with James Young body*

Above *Perhaps the ultimate in regal splendour – James Young's rear accommodation in a Phantom V*

Right *The same car – beautifully balanced for a car so large. Perhaps only Rolls-Royce and the traditional English body builder can build such a car*

Long-wheelbase types were available as Rolls-Royces or as Bentleys. This, in fact, was an SII Bentley, powered by the 6·2-litre vee-8 engine

passengers (which meant that this was not truly designed to be an owner-driver model), though a little of that extra dimension was lost to the bulk of the division. It is no easy matter for a coachbuilder to alter an existing shell which has been designed as an entity, but Park Ward managed it with unobtrusive elegance. Although the front doors were unaltered, the rear doors were significantly longer than the originals and lost their rear quarter lights, and new quarter windows were let into the quarters of a remodelled roof. The roof panel and the floor pan were, of course, rebuilt as necessary, but externally it needs a trained eye to see the difference between the two shapes.

As with the air-conditioning, this was no cheap 'option'. At the 1957 Earls Court Motor Show, a standard steel Silver Cloud was priced at £3795 (or £5694 with British purchase tax), while the

Far left *Rolls-Royce's Phantom VI is an altogether very special car. This 'standard' bodied car is still very rare and fearfully expensive—both as they should be*

Not quite as commonplace (by Rolls-Royce standards) as it might seem. This was not only a long-wheelbase chassis, but it was a four-door Cabriolet version. A very desirable Rolls-Royce, even by those high standards

chassis price *alone* of the long-wheelbase model was £2745 (basic), and that of the complete long-wheelbase car was £4595 (basic), or £6894 with purchase tax. As with the standard steel cars, refrigeration and power-assisted steering were optional extras.

It goes without saying that even in this price class, sales of long wheelbase cars were restricted. In the next eight years, a total of 673 Rolls-Royces and 124 Bentleys were built on this chassis, mostly with standard steel type coachwork (i.e. Park Ward modified), but also with entirely special styles from concerns like James Young and Hooper.

To look after the steadily increasing weight of the coachbuilt cars, to provide for the extra power needed by extra equipment like refrigeration, and to keep abreast of their competition, the Company made two important changes to the six-cylinder engine in its last four seasons in which it was used

A Silver Cloud series III, after undergoing the indignity of a crash test. Even Rolls-Royces, it seems, are not perfect, for one of the four headlamps no longer works!

in this model range. Because there was no further practical way of increasing the capacity, this had to be done by substantial engine tuning, which was carried out without sacrificing any of the Company's traditionally high standards of refinement and silence.

From the start, Bentley Continentals were fitted with engines having 7·25:1 compression ratio, compared with the 6·6:1 of the otherwise-standard engine. This was not enough to give the Continental sufficient performance, so from the autumn of 1956 this was replaced by a version of the engine having an 8·0:1 compression ratio, larger inlet valves, 2·0 inch SU carburettors, and acknowledged power increase of thirteen per cent (never quantified but probably from about 158 bhp to the 178 bhp we know to be the final production figure).

A year later, coincident with the launch of the bulkier long-wheelbase cars, the standard engine was modified to the same specification. Late-model SIs, therefore, were probably capable of about 110 mph, or nearly 10 mph more than the original cars.

As I have already made clear in the previous chapter, the six-cylinder engine had reached the end of its useful development life, and was replaced by a brand-new 6·2-litre vee-8 light-alloy unit from the autumn of 1959. The car, along with other modifications, became the SII, and began the second important phase of its ten-year life. The engine's significance for Rolls-Royce has been described in an earlier chapter.

The SII cars retained the now-traditional price difference between Rolls-Royce and Bentley derivatives (in this case that difference was £100). They also inherited several important chassis improvements. Perhaps the most significant improvement was that centralized chassis lubrication was at last discarded, and in its place each greasing or oiling point was provided with a reservoir which required attention every 10,000 miles, or one year, whichever came first.

The end of the production line at Crewe, with a series III Silver Cloud almost ready to be road tested. Even though the SIII's radiator was lower than before, it was still massive and truly noble in its lines

One of the last long-wheelbase models, in series III guise, with two-tone paintwork to emphasise the long and sweeping lines

At the same time, front suspension wishbones which had originally been pressings were re-designed as forgings, while a major change to the steering layout was needed to make allowances for the greater bulk of the vee-8 engine. Power-assisted steering was standardized in any case, and the substantially-built steering box and inbuilt valves were moved rearwards and re-located on the outside of the chassis frame. A typical Rolls-Royce touch was that the original steering column position was maintained, even though the box had been relocated, by providing a pair of spiral gears to take up the discrepancy. The steering wheel itself was smaller but the overall gearing was still very low; technical chief

Above *An SIII Bentley, which in this view shows how the height of the radiator shell was slightly lower than before, and that the line of the bonnet sloped subtly down to meet it. The twinned headlamps were an SIII recognition point*

Right *The facia and instruments of a series III model, actually a Rolls-Royce rather than a Bentley. Technical Director Harry Grylls went to a great deal of trouble to get the operation of switches and other controls up to the best Rolls-Royce standards*

Another view of the drop-head coupé by Mulliner, in which the two-door style evolved by direct conversion of the original four-door saloon's lines. Forward of the screen, the bodyshell is virtually unaltered, and the standard car's wing lines have been retained . . .

Harry Grylls was, at this period, concerned about what he christened the 'sneeze factor' in steering, whereby an over-high and responsive mechanism might react too abruptly to a sudden steering-wheel movement. It is only fair to say that several experienced testers and many owners disagreed with him.

There was one final development of the all-drum braking system. The operation of the clutch-type of servo was speeded up further, which Rolls-Royce claimed to limit the delay in servo response to a matter of inches of car movement after the first brush on the brake pedal. The braking ratio was changed so that the front brakes took more of the effort in stopping what was now a 4500 lb motor car. At the same time rear roll stiffness was reduced by shortening the arm of the 'Z-bar' at the

. . . in SIII form, only the lowered radiator and the twinned headlamps are different

axle end, and it is worth reiterating that such a bar was not fitted to the Phantom V version of this chassis.

Although there was no change to the body style (it was beginning to look somewhat lofty by comparison with its very few rivals), there was a revised facia, and the car could be recognized externally by the black-painted grilles on each side of the radiator. The major body change was a completely revised ventilation system which could either be supplied in normal form or with a newly developed refrigeration installation. Thus, the separate refrigeration system of 1956 had been discarded after only three years.

All the air for the new installation was drawn from the grille on the right of the radiator, and the mass of the heat exchange installation was located in the right front wing, immediately behind the road wheel and ahead of the scuttle. For recirculation of air and for refrigeration purposes, a grille was installed in the body floor behind the right front seat, and complex air flow and heat exchange systems meant that the whole

One of the last Silver Cloud IIIs to be built with a Mulliner-Park Ward drophead coupé bodyshell. The twinned headlamps standard on all cars built after the autumn of 1962 acted as a kind of 'conditioning' to the fact that the Silver Shadow would also have that feature

installation could be used as a heater, a fresh air blower, or a refrigeration unit. It was a recognition of the changing social hierarchy that the original refrigeration's ducting and circulation had been concentrated on and around the rear seats, whereas SII and SIII cars placed their ducting and the major flow of air around the front seat occupants. (Phantom Vs and Bentley Continentals, incidentally, retained the original system). Although full refrigeration weighed about 60 lb, its basic cost had been cut substantially to £275, which in the context of £4095 being asked for the Rolls-Royce Silver Cloud II made a great deal of marketing sense compared with the original layout.

The final important development change came in October 1962, when the SII models gracefully gave way to the SIII. Visually, the most obvious change was that quadruple headlamps were adopted; a controversial point as the rest of the body's lines were not changed. We know now that such an installation had already been chosen for the Silver Shadow project, and even though this car was three years away from launch, there is little doubt that their adoption on the SIII models was a touch of marketing 'indoctrination'. At the same time, incidentally, the height of the two classic radiator shells was reduced by 1·5 in, and the lines of the bonnet were re-raked accordingly. Inside the car, individually adjustable front seats were now a feature (another acknowledgement of the preponderance of owner-drivers), while the padding and shaping of all seats was changed to give the impression of more space; two extra inches had been found in terms of rear passenger leg room.

Mechanically there were few changes, but after only three years the vee-8 engine had its (unstated) power boosted by seven per cent, with a 9·0:1 compression ratio and larger carburettors. Although there was extra power assistance for the steering (maximum wheel rim efforts were reduced to a mere 6 lb), there were no changes to the brakes, and Rolls-Royce's firm statement that 'when we find a disc brake that is as safe, as

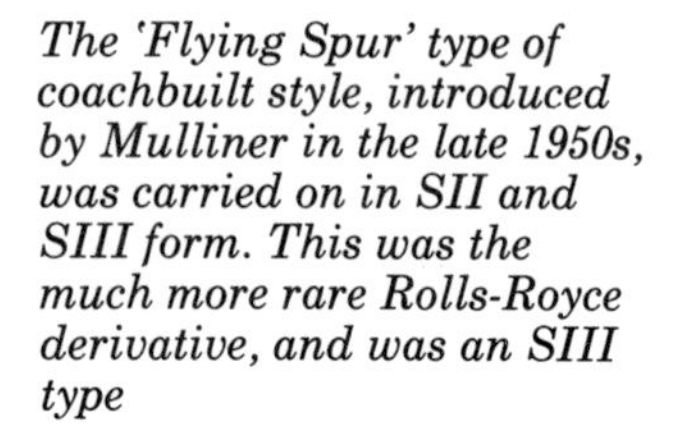

The 'Flying Spur' type of coachbuilt style, introduced by Mulliner in the late 1950s, was carried on in SII and SIII form. This was the much more rare Rolls-Royce derivative, and was an SIII type

The fixed-head coupé derivative of a series III Mulliner-Park Ward drop-head was equally as elegant

powerful, as consistent and as quiet as our drum brakes, then we will use it' began to sound forced. The brakes themselves were large and powerful, but they could indeed be made to fade under the strains of really spirited driving. Those lucky people who purchased Bentley Continentals often did overwork the brakes in arduous conditions.

However, this was the end for the now-venerable design, and Rolls-Royce recognized it as such. Demand for the car peaked in the two years immediately after the launch of the vee-8 engined SII models, but declined steadily as the 1960s progressed. It was not that the car was any less well made than it had ever been, or that its reliability was in doubt (a reputation which it most certainly never earned), but that it was seen to be falling rather rapidly behind the engineering times. Although the new Mercedes-Benz 600—the latter day *Grosser* Mercedes—was no more elegant and certainly no better made than the equivalent Rolls-Royce models, it was absolutely bristling with modern ideas, modern engineering features, and a modern (if Teutonic) style. Rolls-Royce executives must have been relieved, after seeing that car, to realize that their own Silver Shadow—which would be a better car in most respects—was only two years away.

However, this is not to suggest that the standard steel models, particularly in vee-8 form, were sluggards. *The Autocar* got their hands on a standard steel SIII model in 1963, and found that despite its great bulk, maximum speed was no less than 115·8 mph, that it could reach 100 mph from rest in 34·2 seconds (or 60 mph in 10·8 seconds), and dash to the ¼-mile mark in 17·7 seconds, all of which were superior to their own figures recorded on that legendary 1952 R type Continental 'Olga' (OLG 490). The fact that the car's overall fuel consumption was 12·3 mpg was not considered unworthy, especially at a time when petrol cost a mere 4s. 6d (22·5p) a gallon!

For all that, there is no doubt that by almost any standard the SIII of the 1960s was something of a dinosaur—even though it was magnificent in its own way. It was, perhaps, the first time that the pundits came to question the dictum that a Rolls-Royce was 'the Best Car in the World', and began to wonder if the Company could ever transform its image. They should have known better—as the Silver Shadow and subsequent events proved. And while it was possible to be a little less than obsequious to the standard steel cars, the coach-built models were rather special. These deserve special study in a chapter which now follows.

Chapter 6
Coachbuilt cars, and the Phantom V

When Rolls-Royce Ltd. took the momentous wartime decision to market complete motor cars, in addition to supplying rolling chassis to specialist coachbuilders, they reasoned correctly that this would not dismay the vast majority of their customers. They had plans to make and sell more cars than ever before (though this aim took years of postwar shortages to be realized). They could see the social, economic and moral changes which were taking place in the nation's lifestyle, and they wanted to adapt to it. Their decision, however, helped to kill off what was already an ailing British coachbuilding industry.

Right from the start of postwar production, with the announcement of the Bentley Mk VI in 1946, Rolls-Royce made it quite clear that although they would concentrate their efforts on selling 'standard steel' saloons, they would still be ready to supply chassis for special coachwork. Their customers, however, whether imbued with the postwar spirit of 'making do', economically squeezed, or merely apathetic about the whole business, did not rush to assert their own individuality. The most numerous of all Crewe's products in the immediate postwar period was the Mark VI Bentley, of which a mere 999 chassis (or nineteen per cent of the total) received special bodies. More significant, however, is the developing trend—20·5 per cent of $4\frac{1}{4}$-litre Mark VIs were coachbuilt, 14·9 per cent of the $4\frac{1}{2}$-litre Mark VIs, and 13·1 per cent of the R types.

Even as the Silver Cloud series was being made ready for production, it was clear that the demand for coachbuilt bodies was steadily falling though that for Continental Bentleys was strong. Right from the start, however, Rolls-Royce Ltd. made an S type rolling chassis available. In April 1955 the Rolls-Royce chassic sold for £2555, while the Bentley equivalent's cost £90 less. The £90 differential was purely on account of the use of the Rolls-Royce name, and its noble stainless steel radiator shell hid not a single item of mechanical engineering difference.

Although special coachwork had been produced for the previous Mk VI/R type/Silver Dawn chassis by more than thirty independent body builders, Rolls-Royce had to cut down their supplies of S type chassis to a mere handful of concerns because only a handful were still in business. The vast majority of all chassis were delivered, as one might expect, to the two firms of H. J. Mulliner and Park Ward—one of which was already controlled by Rolls-Royce, and the other (Mulliner) to be bought out in 1959—while almost all the others went to James Young, Hooper, and Freestone & Webb.

I should at this stage point out that I have already covered the Bentley Continentals which were entirely coachbuilt, and whose construction was dominated by Park Ward and Mulliner before 1959, and by the combined and increasingly rationalized concern thereafter.

It is interesting to look back to that Indian summer of coachbuilders—to the Earls Court Motor Shows—and see how their numbers (and

Above *Very few of these special coachbuilt Rolls-Royce Silver Cloud estate cars were ever built. The conversion was by Harold Radford, on the basis of the standard steel saloon shell*

Left *Only months after the new S series Bentleys had been revealed, Freestone & Webb produced this coachbuilt body. Not only was the sheet metal different, but so was the treatment of the Bentley radiator, and I cannot believe that Rolls-Royce Ltd truly approved*

Apart from the use of protruding headlamps, this was a very smart rendering of two-door saloon coachwork on the SI Bentley model, by James Young; the general style, bulk, and even the lines were those of the standard product

thus the choice available to the wealthy and discriminating) was to contract. In the year that the Silver Cloud family of models was announced, Earls Court housed sixteen coachbuilders' stands—six of which showed their own interpretations of the theme. In 1959, following the launch of the vee-8 engined SII cars, the numbers had dropped slightly to fourteen makers although of that fourteen only eight could be described as 'custom' coachbuilders, of which five showed Crewe's products. The casualty was Freestone & Webb, but there was also the sober announcement that Hooper (now owned by Daimler) were about to shut down.

In 1962, the year in which the SIII cars were shown, there were still twelve concerns, but Mulliner and Park Ward had been merged, and the Rolls-Royce Company's products were only on

This two-door saloon by James Young is very slightly different from that shown on the opposite page with no wrap-round rear window, and no protruding headlamps

show at two other stands—Harold Radford and James Young. Both these concerns survived to the end of the family's run in 1965.

As with their previous model ranges, Rolls-Royce supplied rolling chassis complete with radiator shells and blocks in place, and with at least the scuttle and normal array of instruments already in place on the chassis. In almost every case, customers wanting a large limousine opted for the Silver Wraith (up to 1959, a design whose chassis engineering was based on that of the obsolete Mk VI/R type/Silver Dawn layout), or for the Phantom V. Coachbuilt versions of the normal Silver Cloud/S series cars were often owner-driver styles, sometimes convertibles, and occasionally something very like the Continentals being built on the Bentley chassis. Occasionally, very occasionally, an estate car

Above *By the early 1960s, James Young's activity was falling away, and many of its remaining productions were formal saloons or limousines. This was a long-wheelbase SIII Silver Cloud, and had a few details of style rather akin to the same firm's work on the Phantom V*

Right *Coachbuilding, but of a different type! Under this very utilitarian skin is a Rolls-Royce Phantom V rolling chassis, but a Bentley radiator is used, and the bodyshell was made merely to keep the wind and rain out. It was a working prototype, used by Rolls-Royce in the mid-1950s*

might be produced, or something (like a Harold Radford conversion) might be built with hunting-shooting-fishing sportsmen in mind. H. J. Mulliner even produced a small number of convertibles based on nothing more special than a standard steel saloon, converted to two doors, and with the top cut off.

By the time the vee-8 engined cars were announced in 1959 the demand for special coachwork had virtually evaporated, and this activity was almost confined to the Bentley Continental. Rolls-Royce's official figures, for example, show that of 2376 Silver Clouds built between 1962 and 1965, only seventy-nine were coachbuilt examples, and 253 were long-wheelbase saloons. Of the SIII Bentleys, there were just two coachbuilt convertibles, seven long-wheelbase saloons, twenty-five 'standard steel' long-wheelbase cars, and 312 Continentals, compared with 1284 'standard steel' SIIIs.

What killed them off, apart from fashion and a change in social requirements, was cost. At the end of this family's run, a standard steel Silver Cloud III cost £4660 (basic) in Britain, compared with £5685 for a long-wheelbase standard steel limousine—and £6750 for a four-door sports saloon from Mulliner-Park Ward. Not even Rolls-Royce customers, it seems, were rushing to pay so much more for the exclusivity of special coachwork.

The problem, too, was that with the laudable exception of the Bentley Continentals, coachbuilt versions of these cars were usually heavier than the standard steel models, and because they were invariably larger they also developed a more impressive inherent headwind. As a double consequence, not only were the 'specials' slower, but they were also even thirstier than the standard products, which added insult to the injury of

This is the very long Phantom V rolling chassis, quite obviously related to the SII frame, and having the same engine, transmission, and suspension components

having to rely on a small, perhaps geographically remote and less organized concern for any body repairs. Even though Park Ward in particular (and others, once they had found ways of avoiding such patents as existed) had pioneered the use of all-metal coachbuilding, which were usually lighter than the traditional ash framing techniques employed for well over a century by the coachbuilding trade, the bodies could not be made as light as a pressed steel assembly.

On cars of this size, with built-in radiators which were, incidentally, a condition of supply, really individual and striking new styles were hard to achieve. Mulliner, Park Ward and James Young in any case had their own chief stylists, steeped in Rolls-Royce lore, well-versed in the needs and preferences of their customers, and all sharing a hatred for the excesses of some European and all North American styling houses.

The most that could be achieved—and was gradually achieved—was that the coachbuilt cars progressively, insidiously, and successfully moved away from the sculptured sides of the standard steel cars, and the definite suggestion of separate front and rear wings. At the same time,

Above *The 'standard' Rolls-Royce Phantom V limousine—no less than 19 ft 10 in long—with seven-seater bodywork by Mulliner-Park Ward. The same basic car is still being built, as the up-dated Phantom VI, in the early 1980s*

Left *This, however, was the original Park Ward style on the Phantom V, which is slightly, but distinctly, different around the tail*

Below left *James Young, too, built a small number of seven-passenger Phantom Vs, called Touring Limousines. This was a 1963 model, with the SIII type of twinned headlamps* the line of the 'front wing' was gradually raised. Thus inevitably a through line from headlamp to tail light would in due course result.

Drawing, no doubt, on their experience in building Alvis bodyshells of original Graber style, Park Ward were first (in 1959) to bring such a treatment to cars for their Rolls-Royce and Bentley customers. Although the style was introduced for the Continental, it soon became available on the Rolls-Royce and 'standard' Bentley chassis as well.

None of these cars, however, were at all significant compared with the Phantom V, which replaced the Silver Wraith in 1959. To those of us who at the time were not 'in the know', this new model came as a considerable surprise, as the Silver Wraith had since 1947, with elegance, unobtrusiveness and great distinction been occupying the top place in the 'bespoke' Rolls-Royce market. It is worth recalling that there had been

In addition to their Touring Limousine, James Young also produced this very distinctive Sedanca de Ville style on the Phantom V chassis, and the car (as the registration number suggests) was once the property of the Jack Barclay group

The rear compartment of the 'standard' Phantom V limousine, by Mulliner-Park Ward, showing the two occasional seats pulled out ready for use

1144 'short' wheelbase Silver Wraiths, and 639 with the optional longer wheelbase of 11 ft 1 in. In addition, one must never forget the very exclusive Phantom IVs of 1950–1956 (sixteen were built), which were strictly reserved for special order and for supply to Royalty and heads of State.

Both these models, however, were based on Mark VI/Silver Dawn engineering, and since this model became obsolete in 1955, it was a miracle that the Silver Wraith survived for so long. In the autumn of 1959, at the same time as the vee-8 engined SII derivatives of the Silver Cloud were revealed, a new model was announced to replace the Wraith. This was the Phantom V, developments of which are still in production now, more than twenty years later, as this book goes to the printer.

39 RR 61

It was interesting and significant that the new model was to be a Phantom, as Rolls-Royces carrying that name had a distinguished record. The original Phantoms, built in Britain and in the United States, had a 7·7-litre six-cylinder engines; between 1925 and 1931 (the American-built cars carried on for two further years), 3453 examples were built. The Phantom II, built only in Britain from 1929 to 1935, retained a development of the same engine, survived the Great Depression, and sold to the tune of 1767 cars. Third, grandest, more complex and most Lordly of all (and—if the truth be told—most troublesome), was the 1936–1939 Phantom III, complete with 7·3-litre vee-12 engine, of which 710 were built, and many of which survive.

For all that, the new Phantom V of 1959 was the bulkiest Rolls-Royce ever built. Although its wheelbase was on a par with that of the Phantom IV, its wheel tracks were wider, and it was longer, wider and higher than before. More important, however, was its chassis, which was nothing less than a long-wheelbase derivative of the standard Silver Cloud/S series layout. A comparative study of Silver Cloud and Phantom V chassis frames shows many similarities and actual common parts at front and rear, though the main side members are completely different, and a cross-braced tubular section is let in to the centre cruciform to accommodate the extra 22 inches of wheelbase.

The same wheels (but larger-section tyres), brakes and suspension layout were specified, though the Phantom V's front track was wider by 2·4 in, and the rear track (by means of longer axle tubes) by 4·0 in. A detail difference was that Phantom V cars, not thought to need such sophisticated aids to roadholding, had no rear axle 'Z bar' location. In all other major chassis engineering respects—the Girling 'Autostatic'

Top left *Probably the rarest Rolls-Royce of modern times is the State Landaulette version of the Phantom VI model, which is built strictly by hand, and very definitely to special order. The chassis of the Phantom VI is unaltered, but the bodyshell is arranged to have a folding hood over the rear seats, and there is a metal removable panel over the rear doors. If such a thing exists, this is the 'standard' shape, and is by Mulliner-Park Ward*

Below left *By contrast this Landaulette, also by M-PW, has slightly different details around the rear quarters, with a larger quarter window, revised sheet metal under and behind that window, and a folding hood modified to suit . . .*

drum brakes, mechanical servo, 6·2-litre vee-8 engine, four-speed automatic gearbox and power-assisted steering—the new Phantom V was virtually identical with the Silver Cloud family. To match the transmission to the much heavier car, to maintain reasonable acceleration, and to ensure the jerk-free type of slow-speed 'creeping' ability which a ceremonial car so often needs, the final drive ratio was 3·89:1, compared with 3·08:1 for the standard steel models.

But if the chassis layout was predictable and familiar, the coachwork was entirely special. In every possible way, the Phantom V bodies were the very best available from the coachbuilding profession. By almost any standards, the choice of coachwork—from H. J. Mulliner, Park Ward, or James Young—was impressive, and all were enormous. Although Phantoms had always been large, this model, at no less than 19 ft 10 in between bumper overriders, was truly extraordinary. Even so, the delicacy of its styling layout, its restrained dignity, and the carefully blocked-out bulk of the very spacious passenger accommodation made it look much smaller to a casual onlooker. It was only when a Phantom V was parked alongside even something as stately as a Silver Cloud that the bulk became obvious.

Although most of us now know the modern Phantoms as limousines, complete with divisions, used not only by the British Royal family but by heads of State and rich people of taste throughout the world, there was a much wider choice of bodies at first. The Park Ward styled limousine, complete with division, occasional 'jump' seats behind the division and a fixed bench front seat may have always been the most popular style (and subsequently became the only 'official' body offered on the chassis), owner-driver saloons (called Touring Limousines), sedancas and vari-

. . . the same car as on page 96 (below), with hood tightly erect, is virtually indistinguishable from the normal 'all-metal' limousine

ations on this theme were all offered by H. J. Mulliner and James Young in early days. The Park Ward car used elements of the patented constructional process (with an all-metal framework clad in steel and light-alloy panelling), while the other cars used more classic and conventional methods of constructing the coachwork. Even Park Ward, however, could not make a light car out of something so truly massive. In 1959, when announced, the rolling chassis alone weighed almost 3000 lb, while no complete car ever weighed less than 5600 lb; by the 1970s, and due to the increased complication of the Phantom VI, this figure had crept up to more than 6000 lb, and the Phantom was easily the heaviest production car being built in Great Britain.

The rear compartment of the Phantom VI limousine has everything one would expect to find in this type of car, including cut glass for the wine, and recesses to hold the bottles securely. The division, here seen partly retracted, can be wound up to the roof lining, or completely hidden away in the back of the seat

Even before the model was announced, several chassis had been delivered to the coachbuilders, and as a consequence there were four separate designs of complete car on show at Earls Court in October 1959. The fourth example was from Hooper, who were almost at their swansong. In these inflation-ridden days it is painful to recall that the basic price of the now-familiar 'standard' Park Ward limousine was a mere £6285 at that time, or £8905 with British purchase tax added. James Young's limousine was even costlier, at £6630 (£9394 with purchase tax).

Almost as soon as the car was properly on sale Park Ward produced the first of a very exclusive type of Phantom V, only supplied to the British Royal family. Below the waistline it was essentially standard, but the entire roof level was raised by five inches (to a lofty 6 ft 1 in), to give more glass area and thus a better view of the Royal occupants. There were glass and Perspex inserts in the roof panel, and the rear section of the roof was a carefully contoured section of clear Perspex. To increase privacy at other times, it was arranged for sliding panels to cover the roof top clear sections, and for lightweight aluminium panels to be fitted over the Perspex dome. These items were normally carried in the boot, and took less than a minute to fix in place. Park Ward's attention to detail was such that, when fitted, they cleared the Perspex by $\frac{3}{8}$ in, thus being usable when the Perspex was wet. As with almost all the Phantom Vs built, though the feature was not standard until the Phantom VI was announced there was full air-conditioning. Only two such cars were built at the time, and are still in use by the Royal Mews. The Company let it be known most discreetly that no order, however pressing or however well-financed, would be accepted from private individuals for this particular style!

While the Silver Cloud was still in production, Phantom V mechanical development faithfully followed its lead. In 1962 the Phantoms were given the higher compression ratio, the modified power assisted steering and the twin headlamps of the SIII cars, though the 2-inch SU HD8 carburettors, were not adopted until March 1964. However, following the demise of the Silver Cloud in favour of the new Silver Shadow, the Phantom V carried on in its own right.

In the meantime, the range of bodies was gradually simplified. From the autumn of 1963,

with the Mulliner-Park Ward merger completed, the 'standard' limousine body became known as the Mulliner-Park Ward style, and continued to be assembled at Hythe Road in London. James Young continued to offer their limousines and touring limousines until 1967, after which that long-established concern (by then owned by Jack Barclay Ltd.) withdrew from the business.

However, from the autumn of 1965, Mulliner-Park Ward began offering a more specialized version of their limousine, the state landaulette (in which the rear section of the body could be folded away, to give the occupants fresh air, and make them more visible). In addition, the rear seat could be raised hydraulically by 3·5 inches. The company was at pains to make it clear that

This, we suspect, was a style not approved by Rolls-Royce before it was built on the basis of a Phantom V chassis. The customer was a Mr Rivers, and the coachwork was by Chapron of Paris

this was by no means a standard-production derivative and never revealed a price for it; delicate hints, however, suggest that it may cost at least sixty per cent more than the fixed roof type.

After nine years production, during which precisely 832 cars were built, the Phantom V was replaced, in the autumn of 1968, by the Phantom VI. The 'new' car was, in fact, little changed. Mechanically there were no significant improvements, except for the use of the latest Silver Shadow cylinder heads, and although no two cars ever seem to have exactly the same specification, they were all now equipped with separate air-conditioning equipment for front and rear compartments as standard. The price, at

Above *In 1960 H.M. The Queen took delivery of the first of two special Phantom V limousines from Mulliner-Park Ward. Known as the 'Canberra' style, these Phantoms were built with specially raised roof lines, which meant that the glass area was considerably greater than standard. At the rear, instead of a conventional metal panel, there was a large one-piece panel of Perspex, which could nevertheless be covered by a supplementary metal panel for greater privacy. These cars, of course, carry no number plates*

announcement in 1968 was £10,050 basic, or £13,123 with British purchase tax.

Production, always to special order at Hythe Road, had now settled down to about fifty cars a year, so it is reasonable to estimate that about six hundred Phantom VI models have, at the time of printing, been sold. The most significant change of the early 1970s was the adoption (for safety purposes) of front-hinged rear doors. Indeed, one of the features of Phantom VI production has been the tiny rate at which cars have been built (and at which, presumably, Rolls-Royce have found it profitable to continue doing so), and of the way in which the basic mechanical specification fell further and further behind that of the Silver Shadow family. Even though Silver Shadows had been given a more efficient automatic transmission (the GM400 unit, with a torque converter and three forward speeds) in 1968, and were treated to the enlarged 6750 cc engines from the autumn of 1970, the Phantoms did not follow suit for many years.

During 1977 some of this leeway was made up—or rather, it would have been if it had not been for delays caused by several strikes. On the occasion of Her Majesty the Queen's Silver Jubilee, the British motor industry joined together to make her the gift of a new Rolls-Royce. There was healthy speculation for some months as to the type of car being prepared, which was finally stilled in the spring of 1978 when a new and comprehensively updated Phantom VI was revealed. This car, though special in many ways, was also the first of the revised Phantom VI models which are now in production.

The Queen's car carried that distinctive 'Canberra' bodywork, with a raised roof line, glass and Perspex panels and a portable 'privacy' cover first seen in 1960, and of which only three examples

Far left *In 1978 (a few months late, due to an industrial dispute) H.M. The Queen received a Silver Jubilee gift of a new Phantom VI, from the entire British motor industry. It was the third of the raised-roof-line 'Canberra' shaped cars—supplied to no other customer—and was equipped with the latest 6·75-litre vee-8 engine and many other new details*

have now been made. As with the other Royal cars, it was a formal limousine, and had many special fittings including a portable dictating machine built into the rear seat folding arm-rest, and the use of seats of different springing stiffnesses to take account of the fact that the Queen is rather lighter than is Prince Philip. The paint finish—in black and 'Royal Claret'—is quite distinctive, and of course the car carries no registration plates.

Mechanically, however, it pointed the way to future Phantom VI models. For the first time, the 6750 cc engine was fitted, and was matched with the GM400 transmission. As this meant that the venerable mechanical friction-type brake servo (which had been driven by a cross-shaft at the rear of the obsolete Hydra-matic transmission) could not be used, the car was re-engineered to take a modified form of the Silver Shadow's high pressure servo braking system, with twin master cylinders and two hydraulic circuits. However, the original car's big drum brakes were retained, with more prominent ribbing of the drums and revised lining materials. For the first time on a Phantom, too, centralized door and boot locking was provided. Because of the mass of equipment in this Royal 'prototype', the complete car weighed a gargantuan 6790 lb, though later production cars have certainly been lighter than this.

Thus updated, the Phantom VI carries on and, at a price of at least £80,000 to £100,000 in limousine form *without extras*, it appears to have no rivals. Just so long as suppliers like Thompson will continue to supply chassis frames, Girling the brakes, and the craftsmen are available in London to construct the exquisitely formed bodyshells, Rolls-Royce will keep it in production. It is in every way a very exclusive 'classic' limousine.

Above *As the 1980s begin, the Phantom VI, conceived essentially in the 1950s, announced as the Phantom V in 1959, and last updated in 1978, is still in production. Only about fifty of these cars are built in every year, all now with bodies by Mulliner-Park Ward*

Left *The interior of the rear compartment of the latest Mulliner-Park Ward Phantom VI, with occasional seats folded away, and trimmed in West of England cloth. On the Royal cars, and with the detachable metal rear panel fitted, there is a much smaller rear window*

Chapter 7
Shadow over the Cloud

I suspect that the team of Rolls-Royce engineers at Crewe, led by Harry Grylls, realized that the Silver Cloud might be the last of its type even while they were developing it. We now know that work on the Cloud's radically different successor began within months of the former's debut in 1955. This was not done because the Company realized that the Silver Cloud was already behind the times, but because it was known that the Cloud was destined for a long life. It was thought that the type of car which would be needed and the sort of engineering to be included in it would have to advance considerably.

Many of the Silver Cloud features would have to be retained. In many ways the Silver Cloud was the epitome of what had made Rolls-Royce cars so deservedly famous—the dignity, the refinement, the remarkably detailed development and the formidably effective solutions to problems of noise, vibration and commotion of any sort. It was, in almost every way, the sort of car Sir Henry Royce would have wished to see produced.

By the end of the 1950s however, and certainly by the beginning of the 1960s, a great technical surge forward was taking place in the British motor industry, and Rolls-Royce was well aware of it. It was simply no longer enough for them to remain faithful to a separate chassis type of construction, rather upright styling, the use of

Here is one of the last of all the SIII models, a Silver Cloud III, with factory registration number, as used in a BP advertisement of the period

230 XMA

After a successful life of more than ten years, the Silver Cloud and S series models were replaced by this new design, the Rolls-Royce Silver Shadow. Although the Silver Shadow used the older car's engine and gearbox, almost everything else about it was new. The most startling innovation, for Rolls-Royce, was that the Silver Shadow was equipped with a unit-construction body/chassis shell

drum brakes, or to the use of a now-unique mechanical brake servo, because they thought there were no better engineering solutions. In 1946 with the Mk VI Bentley, and in 1955 with the original Silver Cloud, they had been right to produce such cars; in the 1960s a repeat performance might have spelt commercial suicide.

Almost as soon as the vee-8 engined SII cars were announced in 1959, and certainly as soon as the modified SIII cars of 1962 were seen to be mere face-lifts, sensitive motoring observers began to think that development of what many consider the 'classic' Rolls-Royce was coming to an end. If not to the same extent as the fitting of the vee-12 engine in Jaguar's E type, it was certainly fair to suggest that here was a fine new engine in quest of a suitable chassis.

No matter how hard the engineers tried (and, to be sure, they laboured for thousands of hours to improve the most insignificant—looking detail), they could no longer disguise the Silver Cloud's sheer traditionalism. In many general ways, of course, the chassis design could be traced back to the Wraiths and Mark Vs of 1938 and 1939, while in philosophy its roots were even more long-established than that.

Even before the Silver Cloud II complete with its brand new 6·2-litre vee-8 engine was on the market, the design team had had to develop split personalities. On the one hand they had to keep in touch with the car which was still in production (and selling, I should repeat, more strongly than any previous Rolls-Royce motor car), while on the other hand they had to begin looking ahead.

Development of the Silver Cloud/S series effectively came to an end in 1962/1963, though the final detailed changes to the specifications were phased-in during the last spring and summer of 1965. Standard steel saloons were delivered up to August/September 1965, and although the special-bodied Continentals remained nominally on the market until the spring of 1966, the last chassis for these cars were delivered to their coachbuilders at the end of November 1965. After that the new car—the Silver Shadow—took over completely at Crewe.

However, as already detailed in the previous chapter, the pedigree of the Silver Cloud was not lost for ever, for production of the Phantom V continued strongly with final assembly in London. Even after this car became the Phantom VI in 1968 there was no slackening in demand. Surely not even the most dedicated Rolls-Royce enthusiast would have forecast in 1965 that the further-developed Phantom would still be on sale at the beginning of the 1980s?

An expert analysis of the Silver Shadow and all its derivatives has already been completed by John Bolster as part of this series of books (*Rolls-Royce Silver Shadow*, published in 1979), and shows the car to be almost entirely different in character and mechanical layout. One important feature, of course, was the unit-construction body/chassis layout. This, on its own, meant that it was now extremely difficult for the surviving coachbuilders to offer special bodywork on the standard mechanical base, for it is much, much harder and artistically constricting to re-body a floor pan (even if Rolls-Royce had been willing to supply them), than to build a complete bodyshell on a separate chassis. As it happens, the only independent coachbuilder resourceful enough to try this was James Young, and these two-door saloons, of which only thirty-five were ever made, were converted from complete standard steel saloons. Every other coachbuilt derivative was by Mulliner-Park Ward.

As a consequence, the many elegant coachbuilt

Silver Cloud/S series cars instantly became more desirable once they were obsolete, and in the expanding 'classic car' business nothing is more desirable than a coachbuilt car of this type. Some, indeed, are more desirable than others, and the Continentals with vee-8 engines are probably the most highly rated of all although the six cylinder cars at a potential eighteen miles per gallon, and no waiting list, are not to be dismissed.

The Silver Clouds and S series Bentleys therefore do have their well-deserved places in the history of motoring in general, and of Rolls-Royce in particular. They have that unique charm of being exclusive enough to be charming and coveted for their reputation and engineering alone, while being well-supported in terms of spares, expertise and loving care from a very active Rolls-Royce Enthusiasts' Club. And in the distant future, when the oil finally runs out, they will still be elegant artefacts to be admired by all connoisseurs of splendid engineering, laudable attention to detail, and supreme quality of construction. How many other cars can match that?

Specifications

Rolls-Royce Silver Cloud I and Bentley SI

Period produced: April 1955 to August 1959

Engine

Type	Six cylinders, in line, with overhead inlet and side exhaust valves
Bore, stroke and capacity	95·25 × 114·3 mm, 4887 cc (3·75 × 4·50 in, 298 cu in)
Compression ratio	6·6:1 1955 to autumn 1957 7·25:1 1955 to autumn 1956 (Bentley Continental) 8·0:1 autumn 1956 onwards (Bentley Continental) autumn 1957 onwards (all other models)
Cylinder head	Aluminium alloy, with six individual inlet ports. Overhead inlet valves, pushrod operated. Side exhaust

	valves, directly operated from cylinder-block-mounted camshaft
Cylinder block	combined with crankcase, in cast iron, with high phosphorus iron 'dry' cylinder liners
Crankshaft	Nitride hardened molybdenum steel, with integral balance weights, dynamically balanced, and carried in seven main bearings. Combined spring-drive and friction-type damper. Main and big end bearings of lead-indium coated steel shells
Pistons	Light alloy, with split skirts. Four rings—three compression and one oil scraper
Carburation	Twin SU carburettors. On engines with 6·6:1 and 7·25:1 compression ratio, $1\frac{3}{4}$ in bore HD6 units were fitted; on engines with 8·0:1 compression ratio, 2 in bore HD8 units were specified
Power outputs	Never officially quoted by Rolls-Royce Ltd., at the time or since. The final engines of 1959, with 8·0:1 compression

	ratio, produced 178 bhp (net) at 4000 rpm, with maximum bmep of 135 psi at 2250 rpm or 267 lb ft torque at 2250 rpm
Transmission	
Type	Automatic transmission of General Motors design, to Rolls-Royce installation, with fluid coupling and four-speed gearing, of epicyclic type. (On early SI Continental Bentleys only, a manual four-speed synchromesh transmission with no synchromesh on first gear, was available at the customer's request. Very few were ever built)
Internal ratios	1·00, 1·45, 2·63, 3·82, reverse 4·30:1. (Manual transmission, where fitted, 1·00, 1·22, 1·55, 2·64, reverse 2·86:1)
Rear axle	Hypoid bevel type, with semi-floating half-shafts
Rear axle ratios	3·42:1 (all models except Bentley Continental)

	2·923:1 (Bentley Continental)
Propeller shaft	Divided type, with ball and trunnion universal joint, and centre support by flexible ball race

Chassis and suspension

Type	Separate box-section steel chassis frame, with all welded joints. Independent front suspension, cam and roller steering, and live rear axle
Frame	Two wheelbases available, of same type, having box-section side and bracing members, plus box-section cruciform member. 10 ft 3 in wheelbase on Silver Cloud and Bentley Continental models. Optional 10 ft 7 in on long-wheelbase Silver Cloud and Bentley S series models from autumn 1957 to August 1959
Front suspension	Independent, by coil springs, double wishbones, with upper wishbone also forming the lever arm for piston-type hydraulic

	dampers and with anti-roll bar
Steering	Cam and lever, with three-piece track rod. Power-assistance optional from April 1956 (export), on home market from autumn 1956, and standard on all long-wheelbase models
Rear suspension	Live axle, half-elliptic leaf springs, lever-arm hydraulic dampers (adjustable from switch on steering column), and 'Z bar' acting as radius arm, and providing a measure of anti-roll resistance.
Wheels and tyres	Pressed-steel wheels with five fixing studs. 15 in diameter and 6·00 in rim width. 8·20–15 in tyres (standard SI models) 7·60–15 in tyres (early SI Continentals) 8·00–15 in tyres (later SI Continentals)
Brakes	Drum brakes at all four wheels; front operated hydraulically, rear operated by combination of hydraulic and mechanical means. Front drums with twin trailing shoes. Rear

	drums with leading and trailing shoes. Drum dimensions: 11·25 in diameter, and with 3·0 in wide shoes. Total brake lining area 240 sq in Servo motor, mechanically driven from gearbox cross shaft, on traditional Rolls-Royce/Hispano-Suiza dry-plate clutch type lines
Bodywork	Standard steel saloon coachwork, pressed and partly assembled by the Pressed Steel Co. Ltd., Cowley, Oxford; finally assembled at Crewe by Rolls-Royce, having four passenger doors. Light alloy doors, bonnet and boot lid panels to save weight; all other panels in pressed steel. No difference between Bentley and Rolls-Royce bodies except in the radiator grille, and in the badging

Major Dimensions

Wheelbase (normal)	10 ft 3 in (312·4 cm)
Wheelbase (long)	10 ft 7 in (322·6 cm)

Track, front	4 ft 10 in (147·3 cm)
Track, rear	5 ft 0 in (152·4 cm)
Overall length	
(standard)	17 ft 8 in (539·5 cm)
(long wheelbase)	17 ft 11·7 in (548 cm)
(Continental)	17 ft 2·5 in (524·5 cm)
Overall width	
(saloons)	6 ft 2·5 in (189·2 cm)
(Continental)	5 ft 11·5 in (181·6 cm)
Overall height	
(Saloons)	5 ft 4·25 in (163 cm)
(Continental)	5 ft 4 in (162·6 cm)
Turning circle	
(standard saloons)	41 ft 8 in (12·7 m)
(long wheelbase, and Continentals)	43 ft 0 in (13·1 m)
Kerb weights (approx)	
(standard saloons)	4480 lb (2032 kg)
(long wheelbase)	4650 lb (2109 kg)
(Continental)	4255 lb* (1930 kg)

(* The mean weight of various types of body)

Major developmental changes

April 1956	Power-assisted steering, and air-conditioning, became optional for cars built for export markets
October 1956	Increased power on Bentley Continental, by increased compression ratio, 7·25:1 to 8·0:1, and 2·0 in bore SU carburettors. P.A.S. and air conditioning now offered on home market cars

September 1957	Introduction of long-wheelbase Silver Cloud limousine (shortly followed by equivalent Bentley SI limousine). At the same time, a four-door 'Flying Spur' derivative of the Continental was introduced by H. J. Mulliner

Basic Prices in Great Britain

Bentley SI rolling chassis	£2465 (April 1955)
	£2590 (August 1957)
Bentley SI standard saloon	£3295 (April 1955)
	£3495 (September 1956)
	£3695 (August 1957)
Bentley SI Continental chassis	£2510 (September 1955)
	£2635 (August 1957)
Bentley SI Continental (H. J. Mulliner)	£4960 (April 1955)
	£5070 (April 1956)
	£5275 (August 1957)
	£5385 (April 1959)
Rolls-Royce Silver Cloud chassis	£2555 (April 1955)
	£2680 (August 1957)
Rolls-Royce Silver Cloud saloon	£3385 (April 1955)
	£3590 (September 1956)
	£3795 (August 1957)

Rolls-Royce Silver Cloud long-wheelbase chassis	£2745 (August 1957)
Rolls-Royce Silver Cloud/Bentley SI long-wheelbase limousine	£4595 (August 1957)

Rolls-Royce Silver Cloud SII and Bentley SII

Period produced: August 1959 to October 1962

Basic specification as for SI models except for

Engine

Type	Eight cylinders, in 90 degree vee formation, with overhead valves, and one camshaft mounted in centre of the cylinder block 'vee'
Bore, stroke, and capacity	104·1 × 91·4 mm, 6230 cc (4·09 × 3·59 in, 380 cu in)
Compression ratio	8·0:1
Cylinder heads	Aluminium alloy, with four individual inlet and exhaust ports. Cross-flow layout, with carburettors and manifold in centre of engine 'vee', exhaust manifolds on outside of engine. Overhead inlet and exhaust valves, in line, pushrod operated,

	with self-adjusting hydraulic tappets
Cylinder block	Combined with crankcase, in LM8 light alloy, with cast iron wet liners. Cylinder bank offset, 1·0 in
Crankshaft	Forged, heat-treated steel two-plane, with integral balance weights, dynamically balanced, and carried in five main bearings; crankshaft damper. Main and big end bearings of copper-lead coated steel shells
Pistons	Light alloy, slipper-type. Four rings—three compression and one oil scraper
Carburation	Two SU carburettors, $1\frac{3}{4}$ in bore HD6 type, on plenum-type inlet manifold
Power output	Never officially quoted by Rolls-Royce Ltd. at the time or since. Approximately 200 bhp at 4000 rpm was developed—a figure estimated from performance of SII models compared with original SI

Transmission

Type	Manual transmission

	no longer available, even to special order
Internal gearbox ratios	Unchanged from SI models
Rear axle	As for SI models
Rear axle ratios	3·08:1 (all models except Bentley Continental SII) 2·92:1 (Bentley Continental SII model)
Propeller shaft	As for SI models

Chassis and suspension

Type	As for SI models, with two wheelbase lengths. Front suspension now with wishbone forgings in place of pressings, centralized chassis lubrication discontinued
Wheels and tyres	8·20–15 in tyres (all SII models except Continentals) 8·00–15 in tyres (SII Continentals)
Brakes	Total brake lining area 240 sq in on all except SII Continentals, which had 304 sq in lining area
Bodywork	As for SI models

Major Dimensions

As for SI models, except for

Track, front	4 ft 10·5 in (148·6 cm)

Overall length	
(SII Continentals)	17 ft 7·7 in (537·8 cm)
Overall width	
(SII Continentals)	6 ft 1 in (185·4 cm)
Kerb weights: (approx)	
(standard saloons)	4650 lb (2109 kg)
(long wheelbase)	4815 lb (2184 kg)
(Continentals)	4255 lb (1930 kg)

Basic Prices in Great Britain

Bentley SII rolling chassis	£2890 (September 1959)
	£3035 (May 1960)
Bentley SII standard saloon	£3995 (September 1959)
	£4195 (May 1960)
Bentley SII Continental chassis	£2935 (September 1959)
	£3080 (May 1960)
Bentley SII Continental (H. J. Mulliner 2-door, or 'Flying Spur')	£5730 (September 1959)
	£6015 (May 1960)
	£6250 (February 1961)
Bentley SII long-wheelbase limousine	£4900 (September 1959)
	£5145 (May 1960)
Rolls-Royce Silver Cloud saloon	£4095 (September 1959)
	£4300 (May 1960)
Rolls-Royce Silver Cloud long-wheelbase chassis	£2950 (September 1959)
	£3100 (May 1960)
Rolls-Royce long-wheelbase limousine	£4995 (September 1959)
	£5245 (May 1960)

Rolls-Royce Silver Cloud III and Bentley SIII

Period produced: September 1962 to September 1965

Basic specification as for SII models except for

Engine	Carburation by two SU carburettors, 2·0 in bore HD8 type. Compression ratio 9·0:1 except for certain export markets, which retained 8·0:1. Power output (never revealed) increased by approximately 7 per cent—perhaps to 220 bhp)
Transmission	All cars now fitted with 3·08:1 rear axle ratio
Bodywork	New SIII Continental styles, and all cars now with four headlamps instead of two headlamps as on SI and SII models
Major dimensions	As for appropriate SII models

Basic Prices in Great Britain

Bentley SIII rolling chassis	£3035 (October 1962)
	£3100 (March 1965)
Bentley SIII standard saloon	£4455 (October 1962)
	£4545 (March 1965)

Bentley SIII Continental chassis	£3080 (October 1962)
	£3145 (March 1965)
Bentley SIII Continental (H. J. Mulliner 2-door, or 'Flying Spur')	£6505 (October 1962)
	£6640 (March 1965)
Bentley SIII long-wheelbase limousine	£5465 (October 1962)
	£5575 (March 1965)
Rolls-Royce Silver Cloud saloon	£4565 (October 1962)
	£4660 (March 1965)
Rolls-Royce Silver Cloud III long-wheelbase limousine	£5570 (October 1962)
	£5685 (March 1965)

Note: Although production of the Silver Cloud/Bentley SIII chassis ceased in November 1965, the last standard steel saloon was delivered in September 1965. The last coachbuilt car on an SIII chassis was delivered in January/February 1966.

Rolls-Royce Phantom V Limousine

Period Produced: Autumn 1959 to October 1968

Basic specification as for Rolls-Royce Silver Cloud SII, except for

Transmission

Rear axle ratio	3·89:1

Chassis and suspension

Type	With extra long wheelbase of 12 ft 1 in
Rear suspension	No Z-shaped radius arm/traction control bar was fitted
Steering	Power-assisted steering was standardized
Wheels and tyres	8·90–15 in tyres
Bodywork	Not supplied by Rolls-Royce Ltd. All Phantom V models were supplied as rolling chassis to approved coachbuilders, notably Mulliner/Park Ward and James Young

Major Dimensions

Wheelbase	12 ft 1 in (368·3 cm)
Track, front	5 ft 0·9 in (154·6 cm)
Track, rear	5 ft 4 in (162·6 cm)
Overall length	19 ft 10 in (624 cm)
Overall width	6 ft 7 in (200·6 cm)
Overall height (unladen)	5 ft 9 in (175·3 cm)
Turning circle	48 ft 9 in (14·9 m)
Kerb weight (approx)	5600 lb* (2540 kg)

* *A minimum figure, and depended on optional equipment ordered.*

Major Development changes

October 1962	Engine changes as for SIII models

1967	James Young bodywork discontinued as this coachbuilder had closed down

Rolls-Royce Phantom VI Limousine and Landaulette

Period Produced: October 1968 to date

Basic specification, until spring 1978, as for Phantom V, except for standardization of front *and* rear refrigeration, and for introduction of Landaulette version of Mulliner-Park Ward body. By this time, the basic kerbside weight had risen to approximately 6000 lb (2721 kg).

From spring 1978, starting with the industry's gift to H.M. The Queen on the occasion of her Silver Jubilee, the following important mechanical changes were introduced:

Engine, bore, stroke and capacity	104·1 × 99·1 mm, 6750 cc (4·10 × 3·90 in 411·9 cu in)
Carburettors	Two SU carburettors, 2·0 in bore HIF7 type, on plenum-type inlet manifold
Transmission	Automatic transmission of General Motor design, Type GM400, with torque converter, and three forward speeds, epicyclic type Internal ratios 1·00, 1·48, 2·48, reverse

	2·08:1. Maximum torque multiplication 2·0:1 Rear axle ratio 3·89:1, as before
Chassis, suspension and brakes	Drum brakes at all four wheels, now operated by high-pressure hydraulics, powered by engine driven pumps (Silver Shadow type)

Basic Prices in Great Britain

Note: because of the inflation experiences in the 1970s, these are quoted only on an annual basis from the launch of the Phantom VI

Phantom V	Mulliner/Park Ward limousine
October 1959	£6285
May 1960	£6600
February 1961	£7050
October 1962	£7305
March 1965	£7875
March 1966	£8700
Phantom VI	
October 1968	£10,050
October 1969	£10,050
October 1970	£10,050
October 1971	£11,150
October 1972	£12,875
October 1973	£13,475

From 1974 the car was not normally listed in price lists, but was usually quoted as 'On application'. By mid-1979, the basic price of the seven-seater limousine was of the order of £80,000, but this figure can be, and usually is, greatly inflated by the optional items specified for this type of car.

Production Statistics: 1955 to 1979

Bentley standard steel saloons	
SI	
April 1955–August 1959	3072
SII	
August 1959–October 1962	1865
SIII	
October 1962–September 1965	1286
Bentley long-wheelbase limousines	
SI	
September 1957–August 1959	35
SII	
August 1959–October 1962	57
SIII	
October 1962–September 1965	32
Bentley Continental chassis (all with coachbuilt bodies)	
SI	
April 1955–August 1959	431
SII	
August 1959–October 1962	388
SIII	
October 1962–September 1965	312
Rolls-Royce Silver Cloud standard steel saloons	
SI	
April 1955–August 1959	2238
SII	
August 1959–October 1962	2417
SIII	
October 1962–September 1965	2044

Rolls-Royce Silver Cloud long-wheelbase limousines	
SI	
September 1957–August 1959	121
SII	
August 1959–October 1962	299
SIII	
October 1962–September 1965	253
plus coachbuilt derivatives	79
Rolls-Royce Phantom V limousine	
October 1959–October 1968	832
Rolls-Royce Phantom VI limousine	
October 1968 to spring 1978 (6·2 litre engine)	311
Spring 1978 to date	Approx. 50 per year

The total number of Silver Cloud, S series Bentley, Phantom V and 6·2-litre Phantom VI chassis built was therefore 16,072.

Acknowledgements

On this occasion our thanks can go to relatively few people and organizations, for all the black and white photographs came from Rolls-Royce Motors Limited through the good offices of Dennis Miller-Williams whose door was never closed to us.

All the colour was taken by Mirco Decet, including the cover, except for one shot and that too came from Rolls-Royce Motors Limited.

Author Graham Robson will already have acknowledged his gratitude to those who helped him—and most of them are at Crewe.

The author and publisher are also grateful to Rolls-Royce Motors Limited for their kind permission to reproduce their registered trade mark on the back cover of the dust jacket.

Index